DAUGHTER OF AN ASSASSIN TURNING PAIN INTO POWER:

A Journey of Faith and Perseverance

A Memoir

Rhoda Banks

DAUGHTER OF AN ASSASSIN TURNING PAIN INTO POWER:
A Journey of Faith and Perseverance
A Memoir

Copyright © 2025 by Rhoda Banks
Written by Rhoda Banks
Illustrated by Orlando Walker
Edited by Ezinne Esther Njoku
Edited by Joe Buccino

All rights reserved. No part of this book may be used or reproduced in any manner whatsoever, without the prior written permission of the author.

Library of Congress Control Number: 2024924593

ISBN: 979-8-218-55782-9

The Rhoda Experience LLC

Dedication

To my two sons, Lil James and Jaylen,

You are my greatest gifts and my deepest inspiration.

This story is for you—so you'll always know where we came from, what we've endured, and how love, resilience, faith, and hope can carry you through anything in this life.

May you walk through life knowing your strength, your worth, and the unshakable love I
have for you.

With all my heart,

Your Mother,
Rhoda

Table of Contents

Introduction 1
Part 1: Shadows of the Past 5
Chapter 1: Witness to a Murder – The day everything changed............ 6
Chapter 2: Daughter of a Ghost.. 16
Chapter 3: The Teacher Who Tore My Words 32
Chapter 4: Shattered Reflection 41
Chapter 5: Pushed to the Edge.. 54
Chapter 6: Hiding in Plain Sight 64
Chapter 7: The Blaid of Desperation... 77
Chapter 8: Sizing Up 87
Chapter 9: He Had Me at Hello 98
Chapter 10: Shacking Up 106
Chapter 11: Choosing to Create Life.. 115
Chapter 12: A Premature Birth... 124
Part 2 Turning Pain into Power 135
Chapter 13: The Strength to Stand 136
Chapter 14: The Other Side of Dorothy 148
Chapter 15: A Son's Turning Point.. 161
Chapter 16: Breaking the Cycle 169
Chapter 17: Crossroads of Parenthood... 181
Chapter 18: It's in the DNA 188
Chapter 19: The Weight of Truth.. 197
Chapter 20: Facing the Hardest Truth 207
Chapter 21: The Winds of Change 219
Chapter 22: A Final Goodbye 231
Chapter 23: Embracing Our Shadow.. 234

Introduction

The first time I saw someone die, I was five years old. I remember the concrete steps of our porch, the way my mother's hands moved swiftly as she rolled our neighbor's hair, the sudden crack of gunshots that would forever divide my life into before and after. That moment taught me my first lesson about survival: in our world, life didn't stop for death. It didn't stop for violence, for poverty, for mothers who couldn't love their children the way they needed to be loved. It didn't stop for fathers who killed people for a living.

I am the daughter of an assassin. My father, Earl Williams Jr., was feared throughout St. Louis as the man people called when they needed to make someone disappear. He was good at it: precise, lethal, silent. He existed only as a void in my world—until that final day when, stretched on small legs like a bird reaching for flight, I peered into the polished casket where he lay. There, dressed in a suit the color of fading autumn, was the shell of a man I never knew, still as forgotten photographs, silent as unspoken stories. I never knew him, but his shadow followed me everywhere, whispering warnings about the darkness that might live in my blood.

I am also the daughter of Dorothy Rogers, a woman whose love was as unpredictable as summer lightning—brilliant and striking when it appeared, but often followed by the low rumble of rage and disappointment. She shaped me largely through her cruelty and emotional absence, teaching me that sometimes the deepest wounds come from the people who are supposed to love us most.

Growing up in Carr Square Village, a low-income housing project in St. Louis where hope seemed as scarce as safety, I learned early that survival meant carrying multiple truths at once. Our community could nurture and destroy in the same breath. The same neighbors who would feed you when your cupboards were empty might also be the ones who would steal from you when desperation hit. The same mother who would carefully braid your hair and match your clothes could also hold a knife to your throat to teach you a lesson.

This memoir is my journey through these contradictions, these conflicting paths. It's about growing up in the shadow of violence while yearning for peace, about learning to mother my own children while trying to heal the child I never got to be. It's about losing my son to the same demons that haunted my family tree. But more than that, it's about the power of the human spirit, about the drive to ensure my inheritance of trauma would not become my legacy.

For years, I've carried these stories inside me like precious and dangerous cargo. They've shaped me, haunted me. They've at once weighed me down and strengthened me. They've taught me that true strength isn't about being unbreakable—it's about learning how to gather your pieces and rebuild yourself, again and again – as many times as needed. They've shown me that sometimes the greatest act of courage is choosing to love when all you've known is hurt.

Through my journey from a frightened girl in a dangerous inner city to an executive in corporate America, from a young mom determined to break cycles to a woman learning to let go of a son she couldn't save, I've discovered that our darkest moments can become our greatest teachers. Every scar, every setback, every

INTRODUCTION

seemingly impossible challenge has been a lesson in the art of transformation.

This is not just my story. It's a testament to the resilience that lives in all of us, the power we have to rewrite our narratives, and the healing that becomes possible when we face our shadows with courage and compassion. It's for everyone who's ever felt trapped by their past, defined by their family's mistakes, or uncertain they could break the cycles that chain them. It's for every child growing up in circumstances that threaten to dim their light. And it's for every adult carrying the weight of generational trauma, wondering if change is possible.

This is how I learned to turn pain into power, how I discovered that even the daughter of an assassin could choose peace, how I found the strength to keep loving even when love felt like the riskiest choice of all.

Welcome to my journey.

With hope and healing,

Rhoda Banks

Part 1:
Shadows of the Past

Chapter 1:
Witness to a Murder — The day everything changed.

I stood on the steps of my childhood home, the echoes of gunshots and laughter mixing in my mind like a haunting melody. I wasn't just visiting my past; I was confronting it. Every crack in the pavement, every boarded window whispered stories of pain and survival. This time, I wasn't running. I was ready to rewrite what it meant to be the daughter of an assassin.

I was five years old when I witnessed a murder.

It happened on a Saturday. I remember because of the weekend routine. I was playing with neighborhood friends in the area we referred to as the "Playpen," it was a bare playground area with concrete, monkey bars, a sliding board and two metal rocking horses. I recall running back to our porch, looking for Dorothy, my mother who was sitting on the step rolling a friend's hair. We lived in a three-bedroom apartment, on a three-door porch, meaning there were two other apartments attached by a wall who shared a porch. We shared that apartment with my mother Dorothy, her mother, who we called Momma, and Momma's two sons, my uncles Freddie, and Curtis. Our apartment was in Carr Square; home to gangs, drug dealers, addicts, teenage parents, murdered dreams, Black kids who barely made it out alive and government-sponsored low-income housing.

Dorothy stood a few feet away from me with a mixed look of cheerfulness and concentration on her face as she rolled our neighbor Connie's hair. I still remember the quick movements of her hands; the way she neatly parted Connie's lengthy brown hair, applied what looked like oil, rolled the hair with pink sponge rollers, and snapped each clasp securely locking each roller in to ensure a certain curl pattern. Connie flinched from pain now and then as she must have been what we called "tender headed," but mostly, she chatted happily with Dorothy, who chatted right back, barely sparing me a glance. I remember that I'd been fascinated by the quick flow of her hands, but it was her face that caught my attention. I looked at it with longing, wanting her to look back at me. But she rolled on as I looked. Eventually, I stood up and walked toward her, forgetting the fun I had just left behind in the neighborhood playpen. She had just walked in the opposite direction, a few feet away from Connie, when I heard the sharp sound of gunshots—the sound was unmistakable because even at five, I'd heard it before. I paused in horror and saw there was a big, scary man standing five feet away from Connie, as he emptied a gun into her body.

I fell to the ground in terror as Dorothy screamed, "Rhoda! Get down!" The next thing I knew, she snatched me up roughly and ran toward our neighbor's apartment door. It was short steps, but my screaming and Dorothy's panic made it seem like the farthest place on earth. The shots rang even louder, and in even more terror, Dorothy banged on the neighbor's door frantically begging for them to open it.

"Let us in!" she screamed. "Let us in!"

"It's open!" our neighbor yelled. "It's open!

But Dorothy was so overcome with fear that she couldn't open the door. So, we cowered in front of it, and Dorothy covered me with her body as the sound of gun shots continued to ring until suddenly, there was complete silence.

Trembling, I kept my eyes closed, afraid the scary man with the gun would see me if I opened them. I don't remember Dorothy carrying me inside our house; I don't remember much from that day. But I do recall the smell of blood and the cleanup from that murder scene the very next morning. I also remember hearing Dorothy tell Momma that Aunty Gert, Dorothy's friend, had gotten shot in the leg while she was trying to run away from the shots. I hadn't even remembered she was there.

"And Connie," Dorothy had added, her voice steady. "Connie's dead. She stole some drug dealer's money. That's why they came for her." Dorothy had shaken her head in disbelief, as if Connie should have known better. "You don't mess with these dudes' money. Everybody knows that. Everybody knows that."

Turns out Connie was getting her hair done because she planned to leave town the next day presumably to avoid facing the consequences of her actions, but they caught her before she could.

"Life don't stop," Momma used to say. "Life don't stop because shit happens." And she was right. Life doesn't stop, not over a few gunshots, not over gruesome murders committed almost daily in Carr Square Village, and especially not over the ones committed by my father.

Carr Square Village was more than just a neighborhood—it was its own world. The smell of Barbecue and smoked meat wafted from Miss Pinky's corner stand, mingling with the sharp tang of urine from the nearby Vaughn's another high-rise housing project.

Kids played double-dutch under flickering streetlights while men exchanged quick nods in shadowy corners. Despite the darkness of our environment, I still often reflect on cheerful moments, and long for the friendships and feeling of family that our community ironically fostered in the shadows of the often-self-inflicted trauma that we all unfortunately experienced.

✱✱✱

I never met my father, but I remember going to his funeral at five years old—a few weeks after Connie was gunned down right before my eyes. I didn't know much about him before then, but after his death, I learned plenty.

My father's name was Earl Williams Jr., but everyone who knew him called him Earl Jr. He was a trained expert shooter for the military and later for one of the biggest and deadliest gangs in St. Louis. Dorothy wouldn't tell me anything about him, but Momma did. She told me my father was the one they called when they needed to clean up or to get back at someone. He had a reputation for being a cold-blooded killer, a reputation that I would later learn would not serve me well as his daughter. Momma used to tell me stories about my father when she had been drinking during the many times that Dorothy would leave me with her. I'd sit perfectly still while Momma rambled on about my no-good murdering father.

"Never knew what your Momma saw in him," she would drawl drunkenly. "He was evil, I tell you. Evil! I don't know why she's into these no-good dude's" Momma would say.

Stories of my father scared me, and the more I learned about him, the better I felt about never meeting him. I'd go to sleep dreaming about him, wondering if I'd grow up to be evil just like him, wondering about all the people he'd hurt and wondering if people would want to hurt me because of him.

Being the daughter of an assassin meant that I was somewhat hated because I would find out years later, as a teenager, a young adult, and a mother, that my father had killed the loved ones of people who knew me. People who, unable to take vengeance on my father and denied justice by his death, looked at me with a mixture of grief and constrained anger. So eventually, when Dorothy spoke about him, she said, "Look girl, be careful who you tell who your father is. You never know who's coming for you or who holds grudges."

And when I pressed for more, she puffed on her cigarette and sank into silence.

Growing up, I came to realize that every family had their thing. That something passed down from mother to mother or father to father, that thing that kept them rooted, trapped, unable to escape their damaged roots. It could be the father who drank too much and beat his wife. The mother who did drugs, the uncle who molested his nephews or nieces, the daughter who was pregnant and unsupported at 16, or the brother who was hooked on heroin. And somehow, it felt like my family appeared to have too much of it. I saw it in the severe mood swings and craziness of my mother, the drunkenness of my grandmother, and the addiction of my uncles. Except we didn't have too much of it, we mirrored most families in our neighborhood; broken in one way or another. We all existed in this cycle, with many not thinking or caring too much about it, not knowing how to break it, and not particularly determined to try. And yet, even in our sameness, I didn't know many kids in my neighborhood who had an assassin for a father.

My father grew up in a neighborhood just similar to mine. But somehow, he made his way into the military, out of it, and then into the gang in St Louis. They sold drugs, ran terrifying robberies, and were brutal to people who crossed them; so brutal that tales of their crimes worked their way into newspapers.

Though I never knew my father, stories of him followed me all through my life. Often stories from people who had no idea I was his daughter. But having been warned by Dorothy, I kept quiet when these stories came up. But I wasn't always lucky. I had my father's face, or maybe I didn't and these people who hated him, perhaps they were haunted by his face, and they couldn't help but find it in mine.

One day, when I was fourteen, I got a job at a summer camp with an organization called SLATE. They helped create jobs and opportunities for underprivileged kids. My supervisor, a man named Val, was friendly and kind. He didn't reprimand us when we took ten minutes extra on breaks or when we showed up fifteen minutes late. We could leave work early if our duties were done. Sometimes, he took time away from his break to come talk to me, and the other kids and I looked forward to his presence. One day, we were chatting, and somehow, we got on the topic of my father. He asked me who my father was, and I told him. A heavy silence followed, and I saw him struggle to keep the shock from his face.

"Earl Jr. was your father?" he asked.

Realizing what I'd done, I nodded very slowly. "But I never met him," I said. "He died when I was five years old."

Valdus remained quiet for a while, and then as if beating himself up for not seeing it sooner, he shook his head slowly and said, "you look just like that nigga."

He walked away after that, and then a few minutes later, he came back and told me I could leave work early. I was delighted by this offer and replied, "Are you sure?" I'd asked. I wasn't done with work. "Go on," he said. "I'll finish up."

When I returned to work the next day, he fired me on the spot. Stunned, I stood looking at him and he stated, "you left the job site early." I started to cry and insisted "but you told me I could leave early!" He replied very sternly "No I did not!"

"You left work early," he said. "You know you're not supposed to do that."

I ran home in tears, and when I told Dorothy, she said, "Goddamn it, Rhoda! I told you to stop telling people who your dad was. Girl, that's why he fired you!"

It happened again when I turned twenty-two. I visited my husband's family, and while there, I met his aunt and cousin. Five minutes after I sat down, his aunt said, "So, I hear Earl Jr. was your father?"

"Yes," I responded tentatively.

"I hate that son of a bitch," she said, her eyes filling with tears. "He killed my son."

The room descended into silence, and everyone stared at me. I wanted to say something to console her, but nothing seemed fitting. Because what do you say to the woman whose son was murdered by your father? So, I said, "I didn't know him. He died when I was five years old."

I realized after I said it that I was trying to absolve myself of this guilt I felt weighing heavily on me. I was trying to tell them I was unfortunate to be the daughter of an assassin, but I wasn't the assassin. I was bound by blood to the man who had spilled so much of it, but I hadn't spilled any. And although no one accused me of murder to my face, I carried the guilt with me for a long time, placed there by a father I never even met.

Still, my father's guilt wasn't the only thing he left me. Once, I almost paid for his sins with my life.

✳✳✳

"Your Daddy almost got you killed; you know."

Momma said this to me randomly one day. I was a teenager by now, one ashamed and afraid to be carrying the genes of Earl Jr. I was tired of hearing about him, tired of the aggravation it brought me, and afraid of what would happen when the next person found out I was Earl Jr's daughter.

"What do you mean, Momma?" I asked in alarm.

We were sitting in her bedroom with the lights turned off. On her dresser were several lit candles. She used to have an altar when I was younger where she burned incense and candles, but she didn't do that anymore. Perhaps it had something to do with Dorothy calling her a witch once.

"I'm damn serious," Dorothy had said, laughing. "You better stay away from her witchcraft nonsense when you are over there."

Still, the incense, candles, and altar are foggy memories of a five-year-old who is not sure what she fully remembers.

"Momma?" I asked again. My father meant almost nothing to me. Still, I was shocked that he had tried to hurt me for some reason. I knew he had murdered many people, but I hadn't thought he would try to murder his own child.

Momma clucked her tongue, shook her head gravely, and said,

"When you were four years old, just an itty, bitty thing, I got a call from a man on the telephone. He sounded like Satan! Then he said to me in a low, mean voice, 'if he dies, so will your grandbaby,' and then he hung up."

"You were sitting on the floor right there, playing," she pointed to the middle of her tiny living room where her old, weathered plastic covered couch sat. "But I knew he was talking about you because you were my only grandbaby who lived with me. The only one who was around me all the time. God knows your Uncle Curtis don't bring his daughter around here. I knew Earl had to have done something evil, and he had. He shot a boy, a little boy, almost shot him dead in a barbershop. And the boy's Daddy wanted retribution for that, and that was you. You were his retribution."

Her eyes bulged as she said it, and I leaned away in alarm.

"So, I cut the phone lines, cut the blinds, and hid you. And then I prayed they wouldn't come take you from me. I didn't do much good for your Momma, but she did me good when she had you. They didn't come for you. They never did. The boy lived, so they didn't come for you.

"Don't tell anybody about Earl Jr. There are people who hate you because of him. Don't tell nobody you are his child."

I went home that day heartbroken. Earl Jr. had ten children from several women in the larger Missouri area. Why was I the child they chose to kill?

When Earl Jr. finally died the way he lived – shot by a sniper while he was coming out of the church – I was one of the kids who showed up at his funeral. Earl had changed, joined a local church, gotten baptized and got married to the daughter of a funeral director. But none of that had mattered. The sniper had been waiting for him on the roof. Earl didn't see the shot coming. He died before he reached the ground.

When the news reached Dorothy, she shrugged and lit a cigarette. She was one of many women who bore his children, and he was no great love. She hadn't even cried, and when her friend, Irene, asked her if she would go to the funeral, she simply said no.

Irene took me. I remember my little hand in hers as we walked to the casket. And I remember the seemingly peaceful look on my father's face as I stared down at him. He'd been dressed in a dark, mustard-yellow suit. There were many people there, enemies and friends alike, but the most familiar faces were the ones that looked like mine— Earl's kids whom I had never met before. Kids who came to pay their respects, kids who, like me, probably never met their father.

At five years old, the funeral was overwhelming for me. Earl had meant nothing to me then. In my little mind, he was a stranger. My life was just beginning, and his had ended. Still, his deeds spread throughout my life, and yet they weren't as damaging as what Dorothy would leave me.

Earl Jr. had spent his life assassinating people. Dorothy had no interest in that; she killed dreams. And for the better part of my life and hers, she would try to assassinate mine.

Chapter 2:
Daughter of a Ghost

I always assumed people hated me because I was the daughter of Earl Jr., but I was certain they feared me because I was the daughter of Dorothy Rogers.

As a child, I believed the world saw me the way Dorothy did: ugly, unworthy, and invisible. But as I stood in front of my mentees, students, employees, and audiences years later, watching their eager faces as I transferred knowledge, and often shared inspiring words of encouragement, I realized something profound—I was never invisible. I was growing stronger in the shadows, preparing to shine.

Dorothy was what people at the time referred to as crazy. Not crazy as in mentally unstable, but crazy as in, "You slashed Tyrone's tires?! Girl, you crazy!" She was volatile and easily triggered, never took any mess from anyone even when she created it, could go from silence to loud to blinding rage in seconds, and was quick to jump to conclusions. I would come to realize, as an adult, that she was, in fact, crazy in a way that was mentally unstable—in a way that required drugs and therapy but that she had no idea, and that perhaps even if she did, she would stubbornly have refused to do anything about it.

Dorothy had me at eighteen on a warm Friday evening. That day, she stood outside with her friends, laughing and chatting like burden-free teenagers. When the first pang of labor hit her, they say she'd been surprised, as if she had suddenly remembered she was pregnant.

"You good?" her best friend, Irene, had asked. And Dorothy's scream of anguish let her know she wasn't.

"She's having the baby!" Irene announced. "Call the ambulance! We need to go to the hospital!"

But Dorothy flat-out refused to go. It was as if the reality of becoming a mother had suddenly become clear, and she wanted no part of it. She stood right there screaming and clutching her stomach until the ambulance arrived and refused to get in when it did. Irene had to beg her to get into it.

Dorothy loved to tell me that my birth was long and painful. That she sat in that hospital bed for hours before those damn doctors noticed her and that they had to force my "big ol' head" out because it was too "damn big!" She said that all the time, every time she needed to bend me to her will, every time I was difficult. She would call me ugly, too, but she reserved that term for when she really wanted to hurt my feelings.

And she would tell me, too, very resentfully that Momma wasn't there. And neither were her brothers; not Freddie the epileptic person, or Curtis the heroin addict, the one who jumped on her, attacking and hitting her every time he got high. I remember fighting him off her when I was four years old. I remember Dorothy screaming, punching, and trying to kick him off. I also remember that Momma was never there. And many years later, when Dorothy talked about it, I saw that Momma's absence hurt her more than Curtis' attacks.

Dorothy and I lived in Momma's house until I turned five years old. Dorothy came and went as she pleased, leaving me with Momma for hours, acting more like a rebellious teenager than a single mother. I grew up mostly in Momma's company, watching quietly while she did chores or sniffling softly because she hated it when I cried aloud. She used to get mad and roll her eyes when I did.

"Girl, stop all that crying!" she'd say. "Get strong. No one's going to cry with you!"

Exhausted from looking after me and her full-time housekeeping job at the local county hospital, Momma would make her way to her favorite bar, Judy's Lounge, and promptly get drunk. So drunk that, unable to make her way home, she'd lay on the street with her dress riding up. Those days were embarrassing for Dorothy and her brothers because they had to pick her up off the ground while people laughed at them. Angry shouting always followed after Momma sobered up. Dorothy would yell at her for getting drunk and embarrassing them like that, and Momma would yell at her for making her take care of me.

These shouting matches were chaotic and hateful, and I stayed balled up in the corner when they happened, sobbing and wanting Dorothy and Momma to stop, but knowing it would go on for hours.

Dorothy often won these fights by cursing louder and throwing things until Momma cowered, ran to her room, and shut the door soundly behind her. On the days that followed, Dorothy would sit in her favorite chair with her head down, one leg shaking, her mood completely black, and her manner oblivious while Momma would drink some more. I would sit at either woman's feet, and they wouldn't even notice I was there. I would cry, too, and neither would console me.

Dorothy got like that, too, on days when Curtis attacked her, and she had to fight him off. On those days, Momma would tremble and defend Curtis. She'd tell Dorothy that he didn't know what he was doing. He didn't mean to; it was the drugs. Couldn't she see it was the drugs? And Dorothy, bruised from these attacks, would crumble into a tiny ball, and sink into even deeper silence. And on those days, Momma would take better care of me, making sure that I ate and was clean.

Dorothy rarely came alive around me, rarely had a kind word or a hug, and rarely laughed or smiled as much. Even though she had laughter that was contagious and a smile that, when genuine, could warm you down to your toes. I ached for her smile, warmth, and laughter. But even at five, I consoled myself with the fact that at least it was just me, it was just the both of us, and I didn't have to share the little she gave with anyone else. But that changed when Dorothy had Rhoshay.

The day Dorothy returned from the hospital with Rhoshay, I burst into tears, threw my little Baby Alive doll on the floor, and raced into the room. The adults had all laughed it off and chalked it up to me being jealous. But I didn't understand why my chest suddenly felt tight and why that small baby, with her cute chocolate face, looked to me like the enemy. Five-year-old me couldn't possibly fathom that I was afraid of becoming more invisible to my mother.

Dorothy was the mom who was never present even when she was sitting just a few feet from me, and now there was a new baby, small, cute, and needy, designed to soak up whatever love Dorothy had to give. The love I was desperate to get. So, for the first two weeks of Rhoshay's presence, I was confused and hurt. I barely ate, and by the third week, I had gone back to peeing in the bed.

Irritated and unable to curb my bedwetting, Dorothy dragged me to the doctor in exasperation and informed them I'd recently started peeing in the bed again, and I wouldn't stop. The doctors informed her that this was normal. That she had a new baby and all I needed was a little more attention.

But the moment we left the hospital, Dorothy bent to my eye level and looked me squarely in the eyes. "Girl," she said sternly, "I ain't got time for this! If you pee in the bed again, I'll whoop your ass."

I didn't pee in the bed again.

Eventually, I got used to having Rhoshay in the house, especially after I saw that she wasn't taking Dorothy's love and attention from me. She couldn't take it because Dorothy didn't have it to give. Rhoshay became a friend, an ally. It was nice to have a sister in the house, someone I could play with when the adults couldn't be bothered with us. Rhoshay joined me in calling Dorothy by her name. Even as babies, we always called her Dorothy. "Momma" never sounded right, and Dorothy never corrected us.

Much like me, Rhoshay barely knew her father. He came once after serving a fifteen-to-twenty-year jail term. Rhoshay had just turned fifteen. He had been surprised to see Rhoshay as if the existence of his daughter was such a strange thing. Then, he'd promised to take her shopping, to buy her clothes and things. But we never heard from him after that because he got murdered a week later.

And unlike me, Rhoshay didn't get to attend his funeral.

With two babies and no husband in sight, Momma encouraged Dorothy to move out. Our tiny apartment had become suffocating, and Freddie and Curtis still lived at home too. Freddie's epileptic seizures were so severe they made him recognized around the neighborhood. Momma was afraid to leave him by himself, afraid he'd go into a seizure, choke on his own tongue and die. It was easier to ask Dorothy to move. Easier, too, because Momma had started dating a man named Bill and Dorothy hated him. Momma eventually moved him into the house, a move that infuriated Dorothy.

But more than all of this, Momma really needed Dorothy to move because even at six, I could see our apartment was being shared by two broken women who didn't know how to be around each other.

When Momma encouraged Dorothy to move out, she said, "I can't leave. I ain't got no money."

A week later, Momma came home from work and handed Dorothy an envelope filled with cash.

"Here," she said. "Go get yourself a house."

Dorothy looked at her, not with gratitude, but hurt. Then, as if to spite her, took the money and rented an apartment just across from Momma's house. We could see Momma right across from our living room window. Dorothy took full advantage of the proximity, dropping us off whenever she needed to. Momma said nothing about this. She wanted Dorothy out, and at least she was.

As Rhoshay grew older, old enough to walk and discerning enough to gauge our mother's moods, she grew quieter, and together we learned to navigate them. Whenever Dorothy got into one of her moods, we crossed the gangway that we referred to as "the lane" to see Momma. But there were days when Dorothy put us out herself, when she'd pack a bag with clean clothes and underwear, shove it in our hands and put us out of the house.

"Go on," she'd say. "Get going. Go somewhere else." And she'd slam the door in our little faces.

We'd walk over to Momma's house, with Rhoshay sniffing back tears as we did. When we couldn't find Momma, we'd sit out on her porch and wait for her. We spent many chilly days on that porch because Momma was at work and Dorothy was in a mood, but we looked cute doing it. Dorothy may not have paid attention to us the way we wanted her to, but she made sure that we looked cute and clean.

Dorothy rarely gave hugs, but she styled our hair like her life depended on it. I'd sit there, my head pulled tight enough to make my eyes water, and she'd mutter, 'At least no one's calling you nappy-headed.' It wasn't a compliment, but it was the closest thing to love I got some days.

And that was enough at the time, until Ray.

❋❋❋

Ray was a heroin addict, a career criminal, and, like Earl Jr., had served in the military. He showed up on the heels of Rhoshay's dad, who by then had gone to jail for murder and rape. Ray slithered into our lives and wrapped himself around Dorothy's ankle, hissing and biting at anyone who tried to come close. And Dorothy, Crazy Dorothy, who once cussed out a man because he looked at her funny, made no move to stomp on him.

I don't remember the exact moment Ray came into our lives; I just remember him being constantly there. Always there with his clothes hanging in Dorothy's bedroom and his place set at dinner—where he ate food Dorothy managed to provide. He never worked and always had his foot on the edge of the coffee table with a bottle of Crown Royal in his hand while his crooked eyes followed Rhoshay and me around. Ray hated us from the very moment he saw us; at least, it felt like it. I didn't like the way his eyes looked at me; he'd narrow them and twist his mouth like he had a bad taste.

It didn't take long for me to realize that he needed Dorothy for her food, home, money, and the tiny little closet space in her bedroom where he kept his stolen goods. We would have a wardrobe full of stolen jewelry, leather coats, silk shirts, shoes, and gadgets, ready to be sold once they stopped being hot. Dorothy never got to wear any of these things, and on more than one occasion, I caught her staring at them with a strange look in her eyes.

Ray came into Dorothy's life about the same time Bill came into Momma's. Like Ray, I cannot remember the exact moment Bill came into Momma's life; I just remember him being there, too. But unlike Ray, there was no hate in Bill's eyes or stolen goods in Momma's closet. He worked, paid his portion of the bills, went to the bar with Momma, and instead of one drunk grandparent coming home, I now had two! As odd as it may seem, Bill with Momma was the first picture of a stable and non-violent male and female relationship that I witnessed. They did things together, like going to the bar to drink or the horse racetrack to gamble. It was such a contrast to Ray and Dorothy.

Sometimes, I went over to Momma's house to be around her and Bill. I never witnessed any affection between them, but I also never witnessed any strife. I liked what they had. As a child growing up, I liked Bill. So, it surprised me how much Dorothy hated him.

When Momma first saw Ray, she rolled her eyes in disgust. From behind her blinds or sitting on her porch, she would watch Ray sneak into the house with his huge bags of stolen goods, and she would narrow her eyes even more.

"Get rid of that no-good dude!" she would say to Dorothy. "You don't need no man like that up in your house and around your girls."

"Mind your business!" Dorothy would snap. "Who are you to give advice about a man when you have that no-good man living off you!"

"He's not! He's a good man! Do you ever hear him knock me around? No, that's your Ray!"

Every time they had this argument, Dorothy wouldn't speak to Momma for days. She would sulk and turn her face away whenever Momma came to check on us. She acted like a resentful and petulant teenager around Momma. And Momma took it for what I see now as penance.

I didn't get it. This irrational hate from Dorothy to Bill, and the consistent anger she spewed toward Momma, puzzled me. It would take me years to realize that Momma had been a worse mother to Dorothy than Dorothy was to me. Momma spent Dorothy's childhood getting embarrassingly drunk. Dorothy once told us in disgust of how Momma got so drunk she slept on the side of the road with her dress riding up to reveal her underwear. "They laughed at us," Dorothy said. "They laughed at her drunk ass, my dirty clothes and nappy hair, but Momma was too drunk to care. We'd pick her up, clean her up and feed her. Heck, we fed ourselves too! Kept the house clean too because her drunk ass didn't know the end of a broom from the other."

Dorothy could never stand a dirty house, mismatched clothes, or single hair out of place. If she came home and found even a toy out of place, it would have her screaming out my name in rage. Her near-obsessive need for cleanliness and order was in direct contrast to her personality. It was as if she focused hard, too hard, on these things because it was easier than facing the chaos constantly raging inside of her.

When Bill made his way into Momma's life, Momma changed. She stopped getting drunk and started to become more responsible and present. She was a different woman with Bill, the kind of woman who could hold her liquor and finances. But Dorothy never got that woman as a child. When Momma finally became the mother she wanted, she didn't know how to be a daughter to her.

In Dorothy's eyes, Momma was playing house with this man, a man who didn't know the wreck she used to be. Why did he get to have all the best parts of her when she had been stuck with the very worst? Why did she have to prioritize and attend to him? Why did she have to love him?

Dorothy hated Bill until he died. He was always the man her mother changed for when she couldn't change for her.

*****

In the beginning, Ray knocked Dorothy around just for the heck of it, just to let her know who the man was. He would slap her for giving him lip or shove her while he walked past just because he could. And Dorothy, who would fly into a rage because we left our toys out, would say nothing to him. Around Ray, she wasn't Crazy Dorothy. She didn't narrow her eyes at him and dare him to say something stupid; she didn't argue with him or point her fingers in his face. She was docile, catering and walking on eggshells around him. It confused my childish brain because though I didn't know my mother, I also didn't recognize the woman she was with Ray.

The first time Ray beat Dorothy fully was on a Sunday. We were in Dorothy's bedroom watching The Carol Burnett Show. We had a record player and TV, and while Dorothy blasted her records every Sunday, from Michael Jackson to Prince, Anita Baker, Frankie Beverly, and Maze, I immersed myself in shows like The Jeffersons,

Facts of Life, All in the Family, Sanford and Son, Different Strokes, and The White Shadow because they made me laugh.

That Sunday, Dorothy and Ray were on the bed while Rhoshay and I sat on the floor, giggling at the TV. Suddenly, I heard Ray hitting Dorothy in the face, playfully, it seemed at first. He hit her the first time, and she laughed and said, "stop, Ray."

He hit her again, the second time, and still laughing, she said, "Ray, stop."

But when he hit her the third time, he was the only one laughing. I turned to look at them, but Rhoshay had covered her eyes and nestled herself deeper into my lap. Ray hit her harder this time, and Dorothy shoved him and yelled angrily, "Ray! Stop it!"

Then he pounced on her. Hitting, punching, and cursing.

"Stop it!" I screamed, and Rhoshay began to cry loudly. But Ray, as if suddenly blinded with rage, kept hitting and hitting and hitting.

I jumped on his back then, hitting him with my little fists the way I used to with Uncle Curtis when he attacked Dorothy, but Ray shrugged me off like a ragdoll, and I fell to the ground, yelping in pain as I struck my elbow on the hard floor. I burst into tears then, but I wasn't sure if I was crying from the pain in my elbow or Ray hitting Dorothy like he wanted to kill her.

Exhausted, he finally stopped, and holding her bloody face, Dorothy ordered me and Rhoshay out.

"Go to your room!" She screamed. "Come on, get!"

Rhoshay, who had been cowering in the corner, immediately stood up and scurried off. But I stood there for a while staring at Dorothy, at her torn lip, bloody nose, and crazy eyes. Until she snapped again, "go!"

I walked out quickly and found Rhoshay sobbing on our bed. Unsure of what to do, I walked to the bed, sat next to her, and cried too. We sat like that for what felt like thirty minutes until mid-hiccup, Rhoshay fell asleep.

Afterwards, I ran back to Dorothy's room to check on her, terrified that Ray had killed her in my absence. But when I walked back into the room, Ray was on top of Dorothy heaving, but he wasn't beating her. They were having sex. I ran back out in horror, my eyes uncomprehending what I had just seen. Then I went back into our room, pulled out a paper and some crayons and began coloring.

Ray beat her a lot more after that, sometimes because he was strung out, desperate for a fix, other times just because. But it was always worse when he was desperate for a fix. Sometimes, we would hear the beatings from our room. One time, I ran out to help, and he screamed at me to "get back in there!" And when I stood frozen, Dorothy had joined in with, "now!"

The beatings occurred so much that I started to have dreams about them. In them, Ray would be beating on Dorothy while laughing, and she would be screaming at me. One day, he shoved her to the ground and beat her like he intended to kill her. All his beatings came from rage, intense agitation, or the need for a fix, but this one had seemed different; the look in his eyes had been one of pure hatred. I grabbed Rhoshay's hand and ran across the street, screaming, "Momma! Momma! He's killing her!" And Momma had run out of her apartment brandishing a skillet.

She ran into our house and shoved Ray off Dorothy. "Get off her! You ugly bastard," she screamed. "Get off her!"

Ray shoved Momma away, giving Dorothy time to get up and race to the door.

"Don't you dare touch her again!" Momma warned, shoving the skillet in his face.

"Get that skillet away from my face, old woman! This isn't your house!"

"It ain't your house either, you worthless loser! You touch my daughter again, and I'll kill you!"

Ray laughed at that and walked to the fridge to grab a beer. He beat her again a few days later because he knew he would get away with it because Crazy Dorothy wasn't crazy around him.

The next time he beat her, I called Uncle Curtis, who, by some miracle, had gotten sober, given his life to Jesus, and joined a local church. He would come over and beg Ray to stop, and when that didn't work, he would try to preach to him. But Ray always laughed. I wanted him to fight Ray, to punch him in the face, to send him packing. But he would come, clasping his hand nervously in front of him, the very picture of anxiousness and humility. And instead of fighting, he would say, "You don't gotta beat on her. You don't gotta beat on your woman like that, man."

In those moments, I wasn't sure who I hated more: Ray for beating on her, Dorothy for staying, or Curtis, who, it seemed to me, was hiding his fear of Ray behind his repentance.

***

Dorothy was the original jack of all trades, trying every single job but never sticking to one. She was a keypunch operator, but before that, she worked for the housing authority serving the elderly lunches. She always found an excuse to quit her job, in sharp contrast to Momma, who worked in housekeeping at St. Louis County Hospital and held down that job for thirty-five years before eventually retiring.

Every time Momma found out Dorothy quit her job, she would sigh in deep exasperation and then come over to talk to her. I remember them standing in the living room, a few feet apart but a world of trauma between them, with Dorothy working her way through her second pack of cigarettes, the smoke making the air around her cloudy.

"This your second job this year," Momma reminded her. "You got bills, Dorothy. You can't keep up and quit every job you get. How are you gonna feed your kids?"

And Dorothy would shrug with false nonchalance and puff some more. She knew Momma would come through, and she was right. Momma always did.

A week or two after quitting her job, Dorothy would take us over to Momma's house to hustle her out of some money. Before we left, she would say, "listen, we are going over to Momma's house to get some money. When we get there, you ask her. You ask her and ask her and don't stop asking her until she gives you money. You understand?"

We would nod eagerly. We did anything to please her; even when it hurt our chest or our palms sweated with anxiousness, we still did it. The alternative was disappointing her. And a disappointed Dorothy lost her temper at a snap or put us out because we breathe too loud.

Just like Dorothy coached us, we would go to our grandmother's house and ask her and ask her and ask her until flustered and exasperated, she would shove money into our little hands and order us to "get!" So, it was always a relief when Dorothy had a job. It kept some money coming in and kept her out of the house, away from Ray. But that often-meant Ray had to mind us while she was gone.

The first time that happened, Dorothy was at her job at the high school punching in night schoolers, and Momma was pulling an all-nighter at her job. Ray, in a spark of pure inspiration, decided to make us dinner. He made a big deal of it, noisily moving around in the kitchen and yelling for this or that when he couldn't find it. Rhoshay and I sat quietly in our room, dreading the moment he would call us. He finally did two hours later. Rhoshay was deep in sleep, and I had smelled the aroma of the food from the room and decided I didn't want to eat it; hot dogs and pork and beans were not my favorites. But Ray thundered our names from the kitchen, "Come get your dinner!" And when we didn't come out, he came into our rooms, woke Rhoshay up, and dragged both of us to the kitchen to eat. I remember scanning his face quickly to see if he had that look in his eyes, the one he did when he was desperate for a fix. That night, he didn't.

Rhoshay sat down quietly at the table and began to spoon beans and hot dogs into her mouth, barely chewing it. She tried to be as invisible and quiet as possible. She figured the more she was, the less Dorothy and Ray would notice her. Some days, it worked out; other days, it didn't.

"Aren't you eating?" Ray asked when I didn't sit.

"I'm not hungry," I said.

He went deathly quiet, and I was reminded at that moment how much I had grown to hate him.

"I just spent twenty minutes making that dinner," he said. "You will eat it."

"I don't like pork and beans," I said.

"Eat the damn food!" he screamed.

"No!" I screamed back. Out of the corner of my eyes, I saw Rhoshay flinch, and I immediately regretted screaming.

Before I could say anything else, Ray grabbed me by the neck and dragged me to the table. He pulled the chair out, pushed me roughly into the seat, and yelled louder in my ears.

"EAT THE DAMN FOOD!"

Rhoshay was crying by now and sniffing, I picked up my spoon and began to slowly spoon the food into my mouth.

"That's what I thought," Ray said, walking away. "That's what I thought."

I didn't tell Dorothy when she came back from her shift or when she came to pick me up from school the next day because I had broken out in hives. It was my go-to every time I was stressed, as I'd been at my father's funeral, or when Dorothy got into her mood and cussed us out, or when Ray beat her and I had to sit in my room and pretend like I couldn't hear. Momma had a huge container of anti-itch ointment just for me and my hives, and I spent many days on her couch sitting quietly, willing myself not to scratch while waiting for the itch to subside.

As Dorothy took me home from school that day, her face still bruised from Ray's latest beating, she mumbled and complained. "Why you gotta break out in hives all the damn time?"

"Sorry," I replied.

"Well, I'm not picking you up next time."

"Sorry," I said again.

Ray would go to prison two years later for robbery, and by then, Dorothy already had a daughter by him, Rayneika.

Chapter 3:
The Teacher Who Tore My Words

With Ray in prison for a second time for robbery, my period arrived. I was ten years old. It was a warm Friday evening, and I was just across the street, playing tag with some neighborhood kids. I had half mind in the game and the other on the road to look out for when Dorothy would show up. There was no telling what would tick her off, but me running around happily playing tag while she returned home from work exhausted was just the thing.

The kid I was with had just caught up with me when I paused at the sudden wetness in my panties. It didn't feel like urine, but I was terrified that it was. So, I stood for a moment, contemplating what to do while hoping my dress wasn't already pee stained.

"Rhoda," the kid said when I made no move to chase her, "you are it."

"I'm coming!" I said suddenly and raced in the opposite direction toward our front door, hoping there wasn't pee trickling down my legs. I got to the bathroom, shut the door, raised my gown, and hurriedly pulled down my panties.

It wasn't urine, it was red. My eyes blinked in confusion. Red?

"Rhooooda!" the kid called from outside.

"I'm coming!" I called back.

Quickly blocking out what I'd just seen, I pulled up my panties. It wasn't pee; I was good. I ran back out and played tag until Dorothy came back home and yelled at me to get my ass in the house.

The next morning, I woke up to prepare for school and banged on the bathroom door when Rhoshay took too long to get out. When she finally did, sobbing wet, I rolled my eyes and walked into the bathroom, pulled down my panties to pee, and saw they were covered in blood. My scream of terror brought Dorothy racing in.

"What are you hollering for?!" she demanded.

"Blood, blood," I spluttered. "There's blood on my panties!"

Dorothy took one look at my panties and back at my face and laughed.

I looked at her in bewilderment. What was so funny?

"Girl," she said, still laughing. "It's your period, and you will have this every month."

She walked out of the bathroom, and I stood there drowning in even more confusion. What in the world was a period? When she returned, she had a long maxi pad in her hand.

"Here," she said, and I took it. "Put that on. And stay away from the boys now. I don't need you bringing no baby up in this house." And with that, she walked away.

We never spoke about my period again.

I spent an hour in the bathroom trying to figure out how to wear the maxi pad, crying in frustration as more blood poured out of me and wondering why and how I would bring a baby home. In the end, I placed the pad on my panties the wrong side up and shuffled out of the bathroom in discomfort, walking like someone had stuck warm, slippery glue in my vagina. It felt squishy and uncomfortable, and wrong. I couldn't play with the neighborhood kids for months after that. I stayed inside my room, terrified of dripping blood wherever I went.

From that day, Dorothy dropped a long maxi pad in my room every month, and in the months when we couldn't afford a pad, she folded a one-ply tissue paper into the shape of a maxi pad and handed it to me.

"This just as good as the pad," she'd say while puffing her cigarette. But it wasn't. In high school, during recess, my period would leak through the tissue, causing the blood to soak through my pants. It was the boys who saw it first, and they pointed and laughed while I covered my face in shame. One of the teachers loaned me a sweater to cover up, and I cried all the way home. School, for me, had always been the place where I stuck out like a sore thumb. I was overweight, shy, and insecure from a mother who kept me from making friends and had convinced me with flippant and hurtful words that I was ugly.

I went to school because I had to, but I spent the entire time feeling left out and alone.

✻✻✻

The year I entered the fifth grade, I was transferred to Central City Lutheran School. Before then, I attended an underfunded, over-crowded public school called Franklin Middle School, run by a strict but loving principal named Mrs. Flowers. Mrs. Flowers used to walk around school with a stick wrapped in tape to whoop us when we got unruly. We called the stick Rattan.

Every morning when we got to school, Mrs. Flowers made us line up outside in a long line, and before each student got in, she would ask you to say a timetable, and if you couldn't, she took away your breakfast. Dorothy mostly kept us fed, but there were days when we had to go without breakfast. On those days, I looked forward to the breakfast at Franklin's. The portions were small, and the meals weren't always tasty, but we ate them anyway.

Anxious about losing my breakfast, I always asked my older friend Wardell to tell me what timetable to say. He would say, say five times five equals twenty-five. Or say three times three equals nine. Mrs. Flowers always lit up whenever a kid got their times' table right, and she would usher them into the breakfast hall with a big smile on her face. But when you didn't get it, she had her Rattan ready to go. And boy, did it hurt!

Franklin was great, but it was filled with underpaid and overwhelmed teachers who sometimes spanked before they asked questions, bought supplies from their personal money, and were too exhausted to give special attention to the students who needed it. So, I was beyond relieved when my sisters and I discovered a Lutheran private school. It was an affiliate of the Lutheran church my sisters and I attended without Dorothy. Dorothy didn't mind that we went to church as long as we didn't try to make her go. The church was called Transfiguration Lutheran Church, and was located in Carr Square, but the private school was located on the West side of St Louis. We told Dorothy about the private school owned by the church, and she immediately had me transferred there. She loved that it wasn't located in Carr Square and was private. In her mind, I would be exposed to a diverse set of teachers and kids who, hopefully, were nothing like the ones in Carr Square. It didn't occur to me then, but in years to come, I saw what she did as her own attempt to make sure I had a much different and positive education than she did. Because of her decision, I met and mingled with kids outside my neighborhood. I spent time at their homes and saw what stable and non-toxic families looked like. I believe that was instrumental to my journey, a turning point for me. It made me realize I could live a life different from Dorothy and Momma's.

In Lutheran private schools, the teachers were not allowed to spank students, and I saw that they were less burdened and more receptive.

There was Jean Love, a neighbor who wore cute white button-down shirts and patterned skirts and always had a smile for me when I would visit her house to talk with my friend, her niece Angie.

"Stay in school, Rhoda," she'd say. "It will take you places; I tell you. Places."

Jean Love had an aura that was soothing and kind, and though I liked Angie, I sometimes went over to her grandmother's house solely to visit her Aunt Jean. Being around her made me more optimistic about adulthood.

Then there was Mr. Dennis White, my 7th and 8th grade teacher, who taught every subject. He made learning interesting and fun.

"You have to learn something to be something," he'd say, and in his class, we were always eager to learn something.

Then there was Mr. Nick, the fun teacher, who still somehow managed to be firm and disciplined. He commanded respect, and we gave it. He would say, "If you don't follow my instructions, it will come with consequences, and that's not a promise. It's a guarantee." But even so, he rarely punished us.

To me, these teachers were the best kinds of adults. They were adults who showed up and stayed. They cared and were consistent, the direct opposite of the adults I had in my life, so I looked to them as the adults I wanted to be when I grew up. And because of Jean Love in particular, I dreamed of growing up to become a teacher. I even played teacher every chance I got, lining up my two younger sisters, teaching them, and even asking for a teacher's desk as a Christmas present one time and miraculously getting it.

Although Central City Lutheran made me hope, made me dream, and convinced me that I could be something other than Dorothy's daughter or Earl's seed, it was also the place where I had my first experience of racism.

Miss Kreger was a White teacher. She wasn't the only White teacher in our school, but she was White in all the ways that were wrong. She was condescending, patronizing, and had a mean streak about her. As kids, we didn't know how to relate to her; we didn't know what we would say that could set her off. In that way, she reminded me of Dorothy: volatile and very easily offended. Still, I loved her class. We read stories and poetry, and I got to lose myself in characters and worlds where I didn't have to wake up to Dorothy's temperaments and sudden rage.

One day in class, we had just finished reading a short poem when Miss Kreger looked at us from behind her owl classes and said, "for your assignment this weekend, I want you to choose a color and write a poem about it."

The entire class groaned.

"And!" Miss Kreger interrupted, "It has to rhyme."

While the entire class mumbled and complained on the way home, I left in anticipation. I didn't tell anyone, but I wrote words in a little green book at home. Words that sometimes made me cry when I read them or as I wrote them, words I made up that made me laugh, words that made me wish I wasn't Rhoda, and Dorothy wasn't Dorothy, and Earl Jr. wasn't Earl Jr. Words that made me feel better on days when the pressure and fear pressed down on my chest and made it hard to breathe.

I wrote these words at night when everyone else was asleep, and the loudest noise was my thoughts. And though I wrote these words with the intention of never having anyone read them, some part of me wondered, what it would look like to have someone else go through my words. I hoped they would say they could feel it because they were just the same as me.

So, as I walked home that day, I thought about colors and how to rhyme them. Red seemed too loud, and pink seemed silly. But then I thought of Miss Kreger and how, when she walked into our class, she stood out in a sea of brown. I wondered what that felt like for her. I wondered if it upset her or made her feel lonely. I wondered what being White felt like to her. And then I looked at my skin, brown and glistening under the afternoon sun, and smiled.

I knew what brown meant to me. And that was the color I would write about. I spent that weekend writing and perfecting my poem. And when I closed my book and put it in my backpack that Sunday evening, I knew I'd written a good one.

❊❊❊

Miss Kreger walked into our class with her owl glasses and her usual sour expression, and I felt my heartbeat nervously. What if she hated the poem? I looked around the class and saw I wasn't the only one anxious. Oblivious to us, she took her seat behind her desk and called our names according to the register.

The first and second kids mumbled through their poems, and we laughed because his was funny. On it went, each kid reading with Miss Kreger putting scores next to our names until it got to my turn. My palms had started to sweat by this time. I hadn't accounted for how nervous I would be. Still, I braced myself and walked my chubby legs to the front of the class. I got there and took a deep breath.

"Go on," Miss Kreger said impatiently. "Read."

I did.

When I was done, the class gave a short applause, and I went back to my seat with a smile on my face.

Miss Kreger came to my seat a few minutes later and glared at me. "You didn't write that poem," she said.

Her presence had always made me anxious. Now that, along with her closeness and hostility reduced my voice to a fearful whisper.

"Yes, I did," I said. "I wrote it at home."

"No, you didn't!"

"Yes, I did, Miss Kreger, I wrote it at…"

She snatched the poem from my hand before I finished and tore the paper into little squares. "You are a LIAR!" she screamed, and I burst into tears.

She dumped the torn papers in the trash as she walked to her desk and gave me an F on the assignment. I spent the rest of the school day crying, and when I got home, I sneaked into my room so Dorothy wouldn't see.

That was my first real recollection of racism. I realized as I got older that Miss Kreger couldn't possibly fathom that a little Black girl had authored a poem like that. It also was the first time I thought of a teacher as mean and terrible—before that, they were the gold standard of adults for me, and Miss Kreger had ruined that, shredded it along with the poem she claimed I hadn't written.

I didn't write any poems after that and forced myself to forget the one I'd written.

Until one day, I wrote a poem on Martin Luther King Jr. that won first place in a poetry competition. I was in my thirties then, and when my colleagues at work clapped and congratulated me with big smiles, I thought of the poem Miss Krueger had torn up. Back home, I picked up a pen and wrote what I remembered:

Brown is you.

Brown is me.

Brown is the color of a little baby.

Chapter 4:
Shattered Reflection

Dorothy had a way of framing every word, every insult, every admonition around my ugly ass head.

"Sit your ugly ass and be still!" she'd say when she combed my hair.

"Get your ugly ass in here!" she'd say when she called me into the house.

"Your ugly ass better not be lying to me," she'd say when she threatened me.

So, by the time I was a teenager, I knew that I was ugly. I would look into the mirror and see an ugly girl that nobody loved, not even her Momma.

The year I turned thirteen was a strange one. I had been seeing my period for three years by then, and some of my friends were just starting to see theirs. Rather than swell with pride at having reached this cusp of womanhood at age ten, this knowledge invoked a feeling of isolation in me. That, in addition to being overweight and bigger than nearly every girl in my age group, made me feel uglier and completely undeserving. I would stare at myself in the bathroom mirror; cupping my breasts to weigh them, tracing the lines on my face, and wondering why I wasn't as petite or pretty as Cindy or Marnie, both my childhood friends or why my skin wasn't as light as theirs.

During my early teenage years, Cindy and I were friends. We grew up in Carr Square together, and from the moment I met her, I clung to her in a way that Dorothy hated. Cindy had more freedom than I did. She was the youngest of ten kids and had a mom who was tired of being strict after the ninth child and mostly let her get away with things Dorothy would whoop my ass for. She also had skin that was brighter, a face I assumed was prettier, and was very assertive and bold. She never took any nonsense from anyone and was very quick to put you in your place if she even felt slightly disrespected. Next to her, I was shy, uncertain, and invisible.

Because of her nature, she was the default leader of our age group, and the girls followed her without question. We used to walk the park together every time Cindy asked us to. We never asked where we were going. If Cindy said to walk the park, we did. And at that age, nobody followed her more than I did. She was one of the few girls who never made fun of me for how I looked or who my family was.

I liked Cindy a lot. I used to go over to her house to hang out with her and her extended family. There were siblings, cousins, nieces, and nephews. It was fun. I liked the freedom there; it contrasted with the strictness Dorothy imposed in our house. I also liked Cindy because sometimes, when we walked in the park, we would sit and talk about the men we would marry. How they would love us and take care of us. How they wouldn't beat us. How they would be kind and gentle.

"And fiiiiine!" Cindy would say, laughing.

"So fiiiiine!" I would agree, laughing back.

But even with our bond, I was insecure around her and a little jealous because every time the boys walked up to us to talk to her, they acted like I wasn't even there. Still, I followed her around because I hoped that somehow her beauty and confidence would rub off on me. All the boys in our neighborhood fancied the light-skinned girls, and me, with my dark, chocolate skin, wasn't pretty enough for them. So, I followed her because maybe the boys would think I was pretty standing next to her, and even if they didn't think so, maybe they would want to be friends because Cindy was my friend.

Dorothy was having none of that.

I realized then it wasn't that she hated me being friends with Cindy; she hated the freedom Cindy had because she thought it would directly influence my behavior. But what she hated most of all was how I followed Cindy like I had no mind of my own.

"Girl!" she'd snap angrily. "I don't want to see you with that Cindy! She and her yellow skin. Her Momma don't know where she is half the time! You better stay away from her! I don't want you bringing any babies up in this house!"

I said nothing when Dorothy said this. Unless you were Ray, you didn't talk back to Dorothy. The one time when Rhoshay did it as a teenager, she threw her against the wall and tried to fight her like a man.

I always stayed quiet until Dorothy left my room, and after that, I'd wait for her cigarette smoke to clear. That was the theme of my life for the longest time; always waiting for Dorothy to give me something, or say something, or do something to show me her love for me wasn't just in my imagination. Because Dorothy forbade me from hanging out with Cindy, I snuck around to see her or waited till night to talk to her on the phone. In some way, Cindy provided me with something I felt was lacking in my life at the time: genuine care and encouragement. My sisters and I often got bullied at home by Dorothy, but Cindy defended me from bullies when she could. Momma and Dorothy didn't raise us to give or receive encouragement, but Cindy, in her way, was able to provide me with encouragement and a little confidence.

I liked having that. I liked feeling confident and hopeful, so of course, I wanted to stay friends with someone who often gave me that.

Because I worked at the SLATE summer program and was able to afford my own phone bill, Cindy and I spent hours on the phone. On one of our many phone calls, Cindy told me with a giggle that she had a boyfriend. I remember gasping in shock because it was completely scandalous to me. The very thought of having a boyfriend filled me with dread. Dorothy would kill me.

Cindy had laughed at my alarm and then offered to set me up. And when that further alarmed me, she assured me all we'd do was talk on the phone. On the phone it sounded safe so I agreed and then began to think up ways to make sure Dorothy never found out.

The next day, while we walked the park, Cindy told me she had given my number to a boy named Mike. And I smiled with pleasure for the rest of our walk.

✱✱✱

Mike and I started talking on the phone every day.

I would wait for everyone in the house to fall asleep and then wait for Mike to call me, and he always did, without fail. We would exchange stories about school and laugh about our teachers. He went to the public school, and I went to Lutheran, so we never saw each other. But the more we talked, the more I liked him, and soon, he became a good secret, something Dorothy couldn't ruin.

Now, every time I walked the park with Cindy and her friends, and they talked about boys, I had something to say, too. I'd tell them how fine Mike sounded over the phone. How he made me laugh and how he was really smart too.

"You don't even know what he looks like," they would say, laughing.

"He's fine!" I would counter. "Right, Cindy?"

"Hell yes!" she would say, and we would all laugh.

That feeling, having them laugh with me and not at me, was exhilarating and warm. All my life, especially in school and even at home, I had people laughing at me. But here, in this circle for the first time, I had kids like me laughing *with* me. It was the greatest feeling.

One night, Mike and I were on the phone, and he suddenly asked, "what kind of candy do you like?"

"Banana-flavored taffy," I said.

"I'll bring you some when we meet," he said.

I giggled. "Really?"

"Yeah," he replied confidently like he worked at a factory filled with banana-flavored taffy.

That night, after we hung up, I went into the bathroom, ran my hands through my chubby face, and caressed my fat stomach while wondering what Mike would say when he saw me for the first time.

Would he be upset that I didn't look like Cindy? Could I look like Cindy? Could I make my skin lighter somehow? Make myself thinner? Make my features more delicate?

I think about that little girl now, standing in front of the mirror hating what she looked like, desperately wanting to change and wondering if anyone would ever love her as she was, and I want to hug her and tell her it does get better. That she gets to a point where she doesn't hate her body, where she starts to believe she's beautiful. I want her to know she finds someone who loves every pound of her, and really, all she needed to do was love herself first. I want to wipe her tears at night and tell her she's beautiful because she is. Always will be.

The week Mike finally asked me to see me, I was a nervous wreck. I worried about what he would say when he saw me, but I worried especially about Dorothy.

What if she found out? What if she was right, and my ass somehow brought a baby home?

Cindy was very encouraging. "Make sure to wear something pretty," she said. "We can ride our bikes to his neighborhood after school."

On the day of the meeting, I dressed very carefully, matching a pair of blue jeans to a floral top Dorothy had gotten me. At this time, I had enough pocket money from my job at the Summer Camp to buy myself some clothes. But I opted to wear something Dorothy had bought me. She had this thing where she made sure all our clothes were pretty and matched. It was the one thing about her I could count on. We could be out of groceries, and toiletries, but our outfits and hair always shone.

Cindy and I got our bikes and raced to Mike's house on the north side of St Louis. We chatted animatedly as we rode, and I hoped our mindless talk would hide my nervousness. When we got to Mike's house, Cindy hung back and directed me to the door. "Go on," she said. "Don't be shy."

I got off my bike, heaved a deep sigh, walked to the door, and knocked twice.

Mike was the one who opened the door. I had never seen him before, but I could tell it was him. And he was fine, like I imagined.

His skin was deep chocolate, and his soft, curly hair was in plaits. He looked just like the boy I'd been dreaming about for weeks.

"Hi," I greeted, my heart pounding and pounding and pounding.

But he gave me a once-over and slammed the door in my face. "Eww," he said behind the door. "She ugly."

I turned, ran to my bike, got on, and sped away like my life depended on it.

I could hear Cindy behind me, asking me to wait up. But I didn't, I couldn't. I didn't stop riding until I got home.

I believed I was ugly. I believed that with every fiber of my being. I went to sleep thinking about it. I avoided mirrors because I couldn't bear to see. But all those weeks talking to Mike had made me hope, had forced some parts of me to hope Dorothy was lying and I was pretty, not beautiful in the way Cindy was, but pretty enough to be liked by a boy. But when Mike shut that door in my face, I felt that hope go out with a flicker.

And it forced me to remember in harrowing detail the time Cindy and I had walked to the playpen at the top of Carver Lane and saw that someone had painted very boldly on the ground, 'Cindy is a Fish and Rhoda is a Booger Bear.' Cindy angrily went home, got a can of spray paint, and sprayed over the words. Cindy hadn't been as upset as I was, I could tell. And though she'd spray painted over them, the words had remained etched in my heart.

And the time I was playing outside of our house alone on the front porch, and a friend of Dorothy's named Cookie walked deliberately to me, bent down, looked me in the eyes, and said, "you are an ugly little girl. And don't you forget that."

And I never did.

I couldn't if I wanted to because Dorothy often reinforced that. So, as I went to sleep that night with tears in my eyes, I wondered why I thought cute Mike would look at me and think differently.

❊❊❊

Ray stalked the house after he came back from prison, his shady eyes darting this way and that when he was high. I'd see him walk past my bedroom, and hurriedly stand up, to shut the door. I did that more often after he walked silently into my room one day while I was on the phone. I was lying on the bed, with the phone to my ear, chatting away. When I turned around, the look in his eyes told me he'd been staring for a while. I froze in fear, and when I found my voice, I asked with all the bravado I could muster, "what?"

And he gave me a slow, lingering look that felt like worms crawling over my skin, turned around slowly, and walked away. I kept my door firmly shut after that, especially on the days when Dorothy worked overnight. But I couldn't bear to keep it shut when he beat her. I always found myself rushing into the room to try and save her. But I always came back with a physical bruise that healed eventually and an emotional one that stuck to my chest with weighty force.

Every time he beat her, Dorothy woke up the next day and acted like nothing happened, like he hadn't tried to kill her while we watched. She would move around the house, cleaning and cooking and serving, acting normal, too normal, as if the pretense of normalcy would make us unlikely to remember our actual reality. I see her pretense for what it was now: a survival tactic. It was easier to pretend and forget, especially because she did not have the strength and the wisdom it took to get out of the situation.

Still, there were days after the beatings when she woke up, sullen and quiet, tucked away in her favorite chair, with one hand holding her chin up and her left leg shaking, completely shutting us out. Even Ray didn't go near her during those moments. He could even see she wasn't there.

***

As a young teenager, I went through embarrassing moments that made me want to die. From Mike's rejection to my uncle Freddie seizing in the middle of the neighborhood while we walked home, to getting stained with my period in the middle of a school day, to having people recoil in horror when they found out I was Earl Jr.'s daughter.

But there's one core memory seared in my brain, and that's Dorothy's naked pictures.

I had a friend Tonya, who lived next door. One day, we were playing jump rope a few feet from our house when Tonya paused suddenly and said, "my brother has a naked picture of your Momma."

I looked at her in confusion. "What?"

"He's got pictures of your Momma naked all over," she giggled.

"That's a lie!" I shouted.

"It's true! My brother said your Momma is a whore."

"Your brother is a liar!"

"He's not! Your Momma stood like this in one of them." She demonstrated a stance I'd seen Dorothy take many times, and I froze in horror. Feeling nauseous, I turned away from her. The thoughts in my head spun. Had Ray taken naked pictures of her?

I ran away from Tonya, who was still giggling, hoping that she was lying. But the pounding in my chest and the humming in my ears told me she wasn't lying. When I got inside the house, I made my way to Dorothy's room. She was on the bed, fully clothed, watching TV. I paused for a moment and took in her light, golden-colored hair, her ebony skin that covered her slender frame, and her long legs. As she turned to look at me, I stared at her oval-shaped eyes and small pert nose. I'd always thought Dorothy was beautiful.

"What?" she asked when she caught me looking at her. "What do you want?"

I swallowed nervously. "Tonya says Eric has some naked pictures of you."

Her eyes widened. "What?"

"Tonya said…"

She got up from the bed before I finished my sentence and raced to a small brown tin box she had tucked away on the shelf in her small bedroom closet. She kept her gun and a spare key to the house inside the box. We were never allowed to touch it. Her hands shook as she opened it, and her eyes widened more when she looked inside. She shut the box with a bang and pushed past me as she raced out the door. I followed quickly behind her.

Tonya ran into her house and shut the door when she saw Dorothy coming, but Dorothy got there, yanked the door open, pushed roughly past her, and made straight for Eric, who was sitting on the couch in the middle of the living room. She grabbed him by the collar and punched him in the face. His mom, who had been sitting in a recliner on the right side of the room, jumped in alarm.

"Dorothy!" she screamed. "Are you crazy!"

Dorothy paid her no mind. "Where are my pictures, you little shit?! Where is it?!" she asked and slapped him. Her eyes had gone dark and crazy, and at that moment, I feared she was going to kill Eric.

"Dorothy! Stop!" I screamed.

Eric's mom managed to push Dorothy away and stood between her and her son. She was panting like she had just fought off a bear.

"What pictures?" she asked, looking from Dorothy to Eric. "What damn pictures?!"

Eric was sixteen years old, but he spent his teenage years acting older than his age. He walked with easy swagger and bravado. It was funny now to watch him cower behind his momma. I would have laughed so hard if I weren't so afraid.

"WHERE ARE THEY?" Dorothy screamed and lunged for him again. Eric looked from his mom to Dorothy and blurted out.

"I don't got them no more!"

Dorothy's eyes narrowed into slits, and I was thankful she didn't have her gun. Her body shook with anger, and she picked things off the table, off the floor, whatever she could find, and threw them at Eric.

"GET OUT!" Eric's mother screamed. "GET OUT RIGHT NOW!"

Fuming and heaving, Dorothy left.

When we got home, she threw things, screaming and cursing while my sisters and I hid in our room. When it finally went quiet, I thought I heard sobs coming from her room, but I wasn't sure. A few minutes later she came into our room and warned us never to play with Tonya ever again. We were not to speak to any of them; we were never even to look at them.

Even if Dorothy hadn't warned us, I would never have spoken or looked at them again. I was too ashamed to do so.

Later, we found out Eric had broken into our house through the window, found the tin box, took the spare key and pictures, and had been coming into our house whenever no one was home. We have no idea how long he did this. We also found out he had shared Dorothy's naked photos with his friends in the neighborhood and other men in the neighborhood who often flirted with Dorothy. These men had passed it to their friends in other neighborhoods.

For months, I got taunted in my neighborhood. Teenage boys pointed and laughed when they saw any of us walking past, calling Dorothy a whore loud enough for us to hear. We were too ashamed to talk back. Their taunts haunted me at night and made me grow an even deeper hatred for Ray because I knew he had made her take the pictures.

Dorothy stayed angry, and she took it out on us by yelling more than usual. Our house felt hotter and scarier. We barely walked around for fear of running into Dorothy.

In her anger, I hoped that it would be it. I hoped it would be the thing that would make her dump Ray. She had taken the pictures for him, no doubt giving them to him while he was in prison. I'd hoped she would direct all her anger toward him and cut him off from her life.

But she stayed. And two weeks later, in the middle of a beating, Ray pulled the heavy telephone off the wall and slammed Dorothy's head with it. Her head burst open, and she collapsed in a heap as me and my sisters screamed. Ray, on seeing the blood pool under her head, ran out the door. I called Momma and the ambulance and cried as they took Dorothy to the hospital.

"Your mom is very lucky," the doctor said the night we brought her in. "If he had hit her a few inches over, she would have died."

And again, I thought that was it. This would be the thing that would make Dorothy Walk away. There was no way she would take him back again. He had almost killed her.

But two months later, after Ray had gone to prison for yet another robbery, Dorothy walked into the house bubbly and happy, with her friend Renee happily at her heels.

"Hey!" She called us excitedly. "Rhoda! Get your ass in here. I've got an announcement!"

My sisters and I piled wearily into the living room.

"I'm married!" Dorothy said breathlessly and thrust her finger at us.

I looked at her in bewilderment. "Married?"

"Yes. To Ray."

I stood, staring from her to Renee, to the bland wedding ring on her finger. I struggled to piece my thoughts together, but they kept breaking and breaking and breaking. Ray? Ray had busted her head two months ago. Ray was in prison. Ray was a monster.

"You...you went to the prison to marry Ray?" I asked. "YOU WENT TO THE PRISON TO MARRY RAY?!"

"Hey! Don't you take that tone with me!"

"This is a good thing," Renee said, trying to calm the peace. "Y'all got a Daddy now. Look, your Momma is happy. Don't you want her to be happy?"

Anger coursing through me, I ran into the room and slammed the door. Ray had hurt her. Ray had almost killed her! That day in the hospital, while the doctors stitched her head, I'd prayed she'd come back home stronger, kinder, and free of Ray. I'd hoped she would choose us this time. But she had gone to the prison to choose Ray.

Eventually, my anger dissipated, replaced with a heartbreak that had me crying myself to sleep.

Chapter 5:
Pushed to the Edge

To Dorothy, Momma was the negligent mother who was never there for her and who let Curtis attack her when he was high, but to me, Momma was our savior.

Momma only had a third-grade education and had Curtis when she was sixteen. Restless and desperate to establish herself, she left Curtis with her mother and journeyed from Mississippi to St. Louis. Before then, while at home, she worked in the cotton fields with her stepfather, who beat her. A few years later, while in St. Louis, she got pregnant with Dorothy and then Freddie. Dorothy and Freddie barely knew their father, but Curtis' father would later relocate from Mississippi to St. Louis, get married and have kids. Curtis eventually sought him out, and they had a relationship until he passed.

Momma worked hard when she moved to St. Louis, taking odd jobs here and there, struggling to make ends meet.

"St. Louis was very hard," she said. "Filled with gang bangers and thugs on every corner. You could get killed because someone liked the shoes on your feet and wanted them. Still, it was better than where I came from. I didn't have to work in no cotton fields in the burning heat. And there was no White man looking over my shoulder, taking most of my money, leaving me with little while I did all the work."

She talked about ghosts, too. She called them 'hanks.' She used to say:

"Our house was haunted by hanks. So many of them. Dead slaves who could find no peace on the other side; dead slaves who'd been beaten to death."

"I was the only one who saw them," she said. "No one believed me, but they were there. They were there all right."

Then she would go quiet, and I would think of slaves who had no peace while living and still couldn't find any after they died.

Nobody worked harder than Momma, especially after she met Bill and stopped getting shamefully drunk. Every dime she made went into taking care of Dorothy, my sisters and I, and Uncle Freddie. Curtis had left the nest by then, making his way as a repentant preacher. Something Dorothy scoffed at but made Momma proud.

To Dorothy, Curtis would always be the brother who beat her. And it irked her that rather than see that, all Momma saw was a preacher making his way in the world.

Momma was not a warm woman. She hated tears, overt displays of affection, and emotion. She didn't believe in anyone coming to save you but yourself. She used to roll her eyes in exasperation and sometimes disgust when I cried, even as a toddler. "Stop all that crying!" she'd snap. "You need to get strong. Nobody is going to cry with you."

She wanted my sisters and I to grow tough skin, so we'd bruise less when the world hurt us. She never said that, but I could tell from the way she treated us. Not in a mean way, but in a no-nonsense, straightforward, get yourself up and get moving kind of way. As far as she was concerned, you needed to believe things would be okay because that was the only way it would be.

Much like Dorothy, she rarely hugged me or told me she loved me. But I knew she did in her own way because she provided for us whenever she could. I thought of her as our rock, as the one pillar my sisters and I could rely on for sustenance. I knew I could always count on her to come through. Because of that, I never expected or even knew how to ask for anything more in the way of affection. We were not an affectionate family. I never saw her be vulnerable in front of me or Dorothy. Never saw them have a conversation that wasn't burdened with resentment or strife. She always had her guard up, her chin squared. There were things to be done and bills to be paid, and she wasn't about to spend that time talking about her feelings.

However, unlike Dorothy's silence, which foretold turbulence and had us taking cover well beforehand, Momma's silence hid deep secrets and trauma. And although her secrets remained hidden, her trauma seeped into each of her offspring, saturating them so that they took from hers to create theirs.

Momma was not a deeply religious person. As a child, I used to see her light candles and incense and sit in front of them as if in meditation. But the older I got, the less I saw that. Eventually, she started to attend church but never settled on a specific faith. She started out as a Baptist and then moved to Pentecostal when Uncle Curtis became a preacher and started to worship there, and then moved to the Catholic church because she didn't like the many rules the Pentecostal church imposed on her. She loved to drink and gamble, and she didn't need their judgment when she wanted to enjoy her pleasures. With the Catholic church, she could go to mass, come home, and do whatever she wanted. There was also the very convenient act of confession.

Momma used to take me places with her – to Bingo down the block, to the senior center to see a friend, to the annual Kinloch Baptist church trips when they'd go to places like New Orleans, New York City, and Milwaukee, and to work when I was still a baby and Dorothy didn't want to bother with me. Dorothy didn't mind this, and neither did Momma until she took me on a trip where I almost died.

Momma was a Baptist at this time, and I was in seventh grade. The church was organizing a trip to New York. Momma asked Dorothy if she could take me, and she agreed. It was one less kid in the house to worry about.

I left with Momma in uncontained excitement, thankful to be away from chores and Dorothy for a week and to be going to New York! We were going to be staying at a high-end hotel, which was an absolute treat because I'd never stayed in a hotel before. Momma's friend also brought her two granddaughters, and I made friends with them on the bus trip.

During the trip, while Momma conversed with the ladies from church, I went off and played with my new friends. We spent that first day playing and running around in the hotel. It was such an easy time. My day began with breakfast before I sought the other children out to explore and then came back for lunch. On the second day, I asked Momma if I could go play around the pool with them, and she agreed with a very stern, "Be careful!"

And with an excited nod, I ran off. When we got to the pool, we found floating devices, took them into the pool, and began to play with them. We stayed near the shallow side of the pool because none of us knew how to swim in the deep end.

While we were playing, I suddenly slipped off the floating device and fell into the pool. Thinking I was still in the shallow end,

I began to swim, but the more I swam, the deeper I got. I tried to come back up, but the water was too deep for my height. I began to panic when I realized this, then desperately tried to come up for air but went under every time.

My lungs filled with fear and water, even more so when, through the haze of my drowning, I saw my friends laughing because they thought I was playing.

Struggling and kicking my legs, I came up for air and went under again, came up for air and went under again, came up and went under yet again. My arms burned from the pain of trying to fight the water, and then I thought, I'm tired. I'm too tired. I'm just going to stop fighting.

And with that, I let my body go limp.

And just as I felt the water pull me in, I felt a hand pull me back out. I felt myself get thrown to the floor, and a mouth jammed on mine, blowing air into it. The lifeguard pumped my stomach, and water came out of it. I coughed painfully, opened my eyes, and saw a lifeguard looking down at me.

"Are you okay?" he asked kindly, and I burst into tears. My friends were standing at the side, looking terrified, and that made me cry even harder. The lifeguard helped me up, and I ran to the hotel room to tell Momma.

✳✳✳

"That was plain foolish, Rhoda! Foolish! Why did you get in that pool? You know we don't swim."

I sat on Momma's bed in the hotel, covered in a white towel, while she paced agitatedly as she berated me. But I didn't really hear her. All I thought about was the water and how, for a moment there, it had felt peaceful, quiet, and painless. Was that what it felt like to die?

"Rhoda!" Momma called. Her entire body was shaking. At first, I thought it was from anger, but then I looked into her eyes and saw she was afraid. That startled me. Momma was never afraid.

"I'm fine, Momma," I said immediately. "I didn't die."

"I can't take you nowhere no more," she said.

"Momma!"

"I can't! Your Momma would never forgive me if something happened to you. There's already plenty she won't forgive."

I was near tears now. "But..."

"No, girl," Momma said, shaking her head. "And you can't run around playing with the other kids anymore. I need to know exactly where you are at all times. Do you hear me?"

I spent the rest of the trip following Momma around; she never let me out of her sight. The trip was ruined after that. I couldn't sleep without seeing myself drowning, and I couldn't hang out with my new friends either because seeing them reminded me of it. I couldn't get their laughter out of my head either. What really got to me was the fact they'd been laughing happily and innocently. We were supposed to be having fun, and my near drowning had ruined the experience for them, too.

When we finally left at the end of the trip, I was very relieved. Momma didn't tell Dorothy about me nearly drowning, but she kept her promise and never took me anywhere with her again.

✸✸✸

Nobody loved Christmas more than Dorothy. She loved it with a purity that was startling, in vivid contrast to the woman she was all year round. She loved to give gifts to others. I discovered this when I was much younger and asked for a teacher's desk without much hope of getting one, but actually got it. Dorothy had wrapped a red bow around it and stationed it in the corner of the living room, right in my line of sight, so I would see it the moment I walked in. I had screamed in glee, beyond delighted to have something so beautiful as mine. On other days of the year, when Dorothy was Dorothy, when it felt like I was nothing to her, I would look at that teacher's desk and imagine her love for me wrapped in a huge red bow.

No matter how poor we were, no matter how many bills we had left unpaid, Dorothy always made sure we had a good Christmas. We always had beautifully hand-wrapped presents under the tree. Dorothy would decorate the house several weeks before Christmas, and then a few days before Christmas, she'd spend hours wrapping presents feverishly. In some way, I think the joy of Christmas, the presents, and the decorations under the tree were another part of her childhood she was trying to reclaim. Momma didn't care one way or another about Christmas; it was the other days of the year that concerned her.

When Christmas came around this year, I could tell Dorothy was very troubled. She'd been walking around the house moodier than usual, snapping at us. It was even more unnerving because Christmas was the one time we could count on her to make us happy. The decorations were up, but the presents under the tree were lacking.

A few days before Christmas, Dorothy came back from work agitated, as if she had a need swirling inside of her and didn't know how to contain it any longer. Noticing her mood, my sisters and I piled ourselves into our room. A few minutes later, she called me into her room.

I walked in cautiously and felt a wave of pity wash over me when I saw how tired and agitated she looked.

"I'm short on money," she said. "I'm not sure how to buy you and your sisters presents this year."

I felt disappointment starting to creep in, but I reined it in. "It's okay," I said.

"No, we need to go to Momma's and get some money."

"And what if she doesn't give us any?"

"She will. We will keep asking until she does."

She got up hurriedly from her bed. "Get your coat," she said. "We need to go now."

Silently, we crossed our busy street. Even in the cold, there were people out and about, smiling and playing around. When we got to Momma's house, we knocked and went in. She was in her living room when we got there. She looked tired, and not just from work. I could tell there were a thousand things on her mind. Maybe she was thinking about Mississippi and the hanks again.

"Hey, Rhoda, what y'all doing here?" she asked.

Dorothy nudged me.

I cleared my throat tentatively and said, "Momma, we need some money."

Momma sighed with the weight of a hundred exhausted slaves. "I ain't got no money today," she said.

I looked back at Dorothy, who nudged me again.

"Just some money for food and stuff," I said. "It's Christmas."

Momma sighed again, "I ain't got no money, Rhoda." She got up and walked to the kitchen, and Dorothy directed me to follow her. I did.

"Please give us some money, Momma," I said again.

Momma inhaled deeply, and I looked back at Dorothy, who shook her head and nudged me again.

"Momma."

"I told you I ain't got no money."

"We need to get some…"

"Dorothy!" Momma snapped. "Get your child!"

"Give her what she's asking for!" Dorothy snapped back.

"I ain't got no money!" Momma retorted back.

"Well, neither do I!"

I was tired of asking by now. I wanted to go back home, but Dorothy didn't want me to let up. So, just like she taught me, I followed Momma around, asking and asking and asking. Until, with a scream, Momma dashed into her room, came out in a split second, and pointed her gun at me. I froze with my hands up, and Dorothy screamed.

"Have you lost your full mind?!" she thundered. "Put that damn gun away!"

"Get out of my house!" Momma screamed back. "Now!"

We scurried out immediately, with me shaking all the way home. When we got home, Dorothy fumed and paced and screamed in anger.

"I don't want to see you in that house ever again!" Dorothy screamed at me. "Ever! Ever! Do you hear me!"

I was too shaken to reply.

Dorothy still managed to get us some presents, but I didn't care much for them by then.

We didn't see or speak to Momma for months after that, even though she lived right across the lane. On the days she ran into us, she walked right past us. Those months were long and frigid, and though I was angry with her and quite convinced that she hated us, I missed her terribly.

Eventually, Momma saw me playing outside and walked over to me.

"Rhoda?" she said rigidly. "Sorry I pulled a gun on you. I just needed you to stop."

Even at that age, I could tell it had taken her a whole lot of courage to walk over and say sorry to me. I saw it in her stance and in the way she wouldn't meet my eyes. It was the first and only time Momma ever apologized to me.

I nodded to show that I forgave her, and she turned and walked away.

Chapter 6:
HIDING IN PLAIN SIGHT

I never thought of us as poor. Yes, we lived in a house with a concrete-based floor and lead paint peeling off the walls, and yes, sometimes we had to go without basic amenities, but even then, it never occurred to me that we were poor. Because being short on groceries or the light bill sometimes was a norm, and being able to afford them every single time was a luxury.

Also, Dorothy, even in her inconsistencies, made sure we had a clean house, clean clothes, and food. And when she couldn't do that, Momma always picked up the slack. So, in a sense, we always had what we needed physically, but we never had the security or safety of being emotionally validated—of knowing we were fully loved and accepted.

However, when you have lived like this all your life, having what you need but never what you want or having just enough to keep you afloat, and someone or something shines a light on the seeming insufficiency of your existence, if you are anything like me, you want to run and hide because the shame of this realization is just too awful to bear.

This light shone on me when I began high school.

After we graduated middle school, most of my classmates and the few friends I'd made announced they would be going to Lutheran North Private High School. Lutheran North was small, expensive, and in some way exclusive, and the only kids who went there were kids who got scholarships or whose parents could afford it. I fell in neither category. But that didn't stop me from wanting to attend the school. The alternative of not going to Lutheran North Private High School was going to the public high school near our neighborhood or being bused out to the suburbs to attend one of the county schools. I didn't want to do either because I wanted to go to school with students I had been friends with for years in grade school. Making friends for me was about as easy as jumping through a burning circle of fire. I got burned every time I tried, and I was not about to lose the few friends I'd made. So, all through the summer holiday, I thought of ways to convince Dorothy to send me to Lutheran North.

The first time I told Dorothy about wanting to go to Lutheran North, she was sitting in her usual chair smoking. I wanted to catch her in the best mood to reduce my chances of hearing no. But when I asked, Dorothy shook her head sadly.

"I want you to go, Rhoda," she said. "But we can't afford it."

I tried to hide my devastation as I walked away, and it was easy to manage because I saw that Dorothy was deeply saddened about me not being able to go. Unlike us, Dorothy never went to private school, didn't finish high school, and barely got out of Carr Square Village. Her childhood consisted of neglect and the burden of tending to a drunken and broken mother. So, every time she put fancy ribbons in our hair, matched our dresses, or sent us to schools she could barely afford, it was her way of reclaiming the childhood that she'd been denied. I only wish she'd tended to our hearts the way she tended to our appearance.

As the summer holiday ended, I resigned myself to going to the public school close to our neighborhood.

But then, a miracle happened.

Dorothy received a letter from Social Security stating she would start receiving three hundred dollars per month until I turned eighteen. These checks were benefits from Earl's time in the military, and since he was dead, the checks were supposed to go to his beneficiaries. Being his kid, I was one. Dorothy had been stunned and disbelieving. But it was true; it was right there, and I remember with such clear vividity how she had exclaimed with joy and said, "Rhoda! I can now send you to Lutheran North!"

I think about that moment with such fondness now because of all the things that came to her mind at that moment; sending me to the school I desperately wanted to go to had been first. Even more so because we both had vastly different reasons why I wanted to go. I wanted to attend Lutheran North so I'd stick closer to my friends, and Dorothy was trying to give me the best education she could.

Dorothy was so excited she didn't even stop to check how the money had come. Eventually, we found out my aunt, Earl's sister, had submitted our names. The week Dorothy got her first check, she paid my fees to the school and moved us into a three-bedroom apartment because we needed more space with Rayneika being born. While we lived there, Ray got out of prison, got Dorothy pregnant with his second daughter, Rayshaun, and then promptly went off to prison again. Much like our first apartment, this one was right next to Momma. Momma had moved the year before and Dorothy had chosen our new apartment for its proximity to her.

The week before I started high school, I used my savings from my summer job at SLATE to shop for new clothes. Dorothy went with me. Dorothy hated a lot of things, but she loved shopping for clothes. Her eyes glowed as she picked outfit after outfit for me, shoving them in my hands so I could change in the dressing room. Every time I came out with an outfit she liked; she would clap her hands in glee. She got such joy from being around pretty clothes and dressing us up in pretty clothes that it was impossible not to catch her excitement. I smiled and clapped in glee, too. It turned out to be such a good day.

To this day, I shop for clothes like Dorothy, my eyes glowing like hers every time I see a gorgeous outfit. The more I shopped for myself, and even for others eventually, the more I realized my love of clothes had nothing to do with vanity. It was birthed by Dorothy's love of them. Dorothy was not an easy woman to love, and though she bore us, in many ways, it felt like we didn't belong to her the way daughters should belong to their mothers. But loving something she loved and realizing I loved it for me, made me feel like I belonged to her in a special type of way.

The night before I went to school, I slept, woke up, went to the bathroom, came back, checked my outfit laid reverently on the teacher's desk I had gotten for Christmas. I slept, woke up again, wrote in my journal, checked my outfit, slept, woke up, stayed up, slept again, woke up, woke up, and checked the time; it was 3 a.m. I slept, woke up, got down on my knees and prayed, fell asleep on my knees, woke up, climbed the bed, slept, woke up, and stayed up until morning.

When it was time for school, I dressed carefully, packing my braids in a ponytail and taking care not to look at my face too closely as I did. When I was done dressing, I stared at my outfit in the mirror. It matched. I stepped out of the room to find Dorothy waiting for me in the living room, cigarette in one hand, five dollars in the other. The clock was just striking six.

"Here," she said. "You are going to need that for the bus."

"The bus?" I asked. How many buses? Five dollars was a lot. Dorothy never gave us money for snacks.

"You'll need to take three buses to get there."

"Three buses?"

"What? You are the one who wants to go to some fancy high school. It's going take you three buses to get there."

"Are you… Will you be going with me?" I asked. "Just this first time," I added quickly when Dorothy looked at me incredulously.

"Girl, ain't nobody going nowhere with you. I have to work. You better leave or you are going be late. Be careful on these buses, and don't talk to strangers."

She took one last puff of her cigarette, dumped it in her ashtray, and walked into the room to get ready for work. I'm not sure what job she had at the time. I had stopped keeping track.

I took a deep breath and walked out of the house. High school was waiting.

✳✳✳

Going to Lutheran North felt like going to another state. It was so far that each bus took at least thirty minutes to get to its destination. Every morning, I would get up at 5 a.m. so I could leave the house at 5:30 a.m. while it was still dark outside. I would make my first walk out of our neighborhood to the Cass Bus line, looking left and right to make sure no one was following me. On hot mornings, my clothes stuck to my back, and my braids plastered my cheeks, and on cold ones, my teeth clattered as I rubbed my hands and tied my scarf tighter around my neck.

Once the Cass Bus stopped, I'd catch the Grand bus to Natural Bridge Road and then wait on the Natural Bridge bus for another bus that would take me to the front of the school entrance. On snowy days, the Natural Bridge bus didn't take us to the school entrance but instead would only drop us off at Natural Bridge Road, and I would have to walk three miles up the hill on Lucas and Hunt Road in the heat, cold and often icy conditions to get to school. Often, I would arrive panting and exhausted, with the other kids looking at me weird. Many of the kids came to school in their cars or their parents' cars. So, it was always strange and hilarious to find a student trudging up to the school in such conditions.

In my first year, I and a girl I made friends with waited at a gas station for the Natural Ridge bus. Her name was Candance. She was cute and short, and her dimples set off the most beautiful smile. I used to feel so ugly standing next to her, and though we were good friends, I couldn't help comparing my body and face to hers. Our neighborhoods were close to one another, so we often met up at the bus stop. We grew to be close, even standing close to each other to keep warm during winter. We continued like that until the manager of the gas station accused us of stealing and told us to "get out! And go wait out in the cold!" Neither of us had stolen but there was no explaining that to the angry manager.

After the altercation with the gas station manager, he banned us from waiting in his gas station, so we were back to waiting in the cold. We waited that way for weeks until the parents of Nikki, a fellow classmate, invited us to come wait in the car with them. Like us, they were waiting for the Natural Bridge bus. I don't have a lot of fond memories of Lutheran North High School, but being allowed to wait in that car proved to be not just a warm memory but a teaching moment on the power of simple kindness.

I found that classmate Nikki years later on LinkedIn and messaged her to thank her and her parents for that act of kindness. She barely remembered, but I thanked her anyway. It was nothing to her, but it had been everything to me and Candance.

Lutheran North never proactively canceled school, not even when the snow fall included ice, making it near impossible to trudge up that hill on Lucas and Hunt Road toward the entrance of the school.

I remember a particular snow day. It had snowed for hours, and the roads were completely covered. Dorothy had looked at me aghast as I made my way to school, but she hadn't stopped me. Because just as we had predicted, Lutheran North had refused to cancel school. Somehow, I made my way to Natural Bridge to wait for the bus that would take us to school. But, because the hill was covered in ice, the bus couldn't drive through it. Desperate, I trudged up the hill, shivering and almost falling backward several times. When I got to school, they announced over the intercom that school was dismissed due to the weather. When I thought about going back down and waiting for the bus, I went into the bathroom at the school to cry out of frustration.

I think back now, and it stands out to me how this school cared nothing for the kids who lived in low-income neighborhoods and used public transportation. They made no allowances and never tried to level the playing field so we could catch up. Perhaps they felt us being there was enough. I wonder now if it's why I never missed a day of school—if my resilience was defiance in the face of their indifference.

Often, by the time I got to school, I was hungry, and my chest hurt from walking. I did meet my friends from Grade school, but their smiles were polite and distant. They had moved on to new friends.

It was a different world. Fitting in was the currency of survival, and I was so poor I didn't have that either.

***

High school was filled with all the things I didn't have friends, girls with boyfriends, allowances, make-up, lunch money, cute outfits, tampons, attentive moms who stormed the school to demand more attention be paid to their kids, kids with two parents, even more allowances, kids with cars, kids with dreams of going to college.

High school was also filled with things I did have, like zits, low self-esteem, insecurity, loneliness, inattentive moms, kids with one parent, identity crisis, often toilet paper used to create a make-shift tampon, and… suicidal thoughts. We were divided by class but united by our raging hormones and desperate desires to be seen, accepted, and loved. Some had this desire more than others. I was one of them.

During my first month in Lutheran North, Dorothy asked me every day if I'd made friends, and every time I answered negatively, she would roll her eyes in disappointment. Before that, she was very intent on me not making friends in the neighborhood. So, her sudden interest in my social life confused me. Still, I wanted to make friends as much as she wanted me to. Walking down the halls solo was scary, and it left you open to unwanted attention.

Soon, I avoided Dorothy after school because I didn't know how to tell her I hadn't made any friends. I could see how much it hurt her when I said no. I could see that this was something she really wanted for me. Disappointing her was painful. As much as Dorothy broke my heart, I hated disappointing her.

However, a few months later, and much to Dorothy's delight, I did finally make a friend. Her name was Samatra Davis. Samatra was nice. She was the kind of girl you liked immediately because of her outgoing personality. Where other kids at school walked past, making me as invisible as the wall of their false security, Samatra saw me. She gave me a smile the first time we met, and I had to pause and look around to make sure it was for me. Her smile was warm and friendly, the kind you reserved for a friend you couldn't wait to see. Her smile made me visible to the other students as if my form had suddenly materialized, and now people could see me.

My heart accepted Samatra completely because I knew without a doubt, she was the type of friend Dorothy would want me to have. She walked and talked differently than the girls in my neighborhood like she had a proper lunch waiting for her when she got home and had her laundry folded neatly on her bed by her mom. She sounded like the kind of girl who would marry a good man, the kind who would never beat her, who would carry her in glee and excitement when they took their wedding pictures and then carry her over the threshold of their home because he was big and strong. She looked like the kind of girl who would grow up to be a woman who always had money and whose husband massaged her feet when she was pregnant and hungry and asked her if she wanted more crackers. Being near her had given me a sense of possibility like I could be that woman. But now I know I was just desperate.

So, we spent time together until it was impossible to see Samatra without Rhoda.

The next time Dorothy asked me if I had made friends, I nodded with tentative excitement as if acknowledging it would somehow make our friendship dissolve and send me back into invisibility.

"Good," Dorothy responded with a big smile. "Good for you."

∗∗∗

"Do you want to come over to my house for a sleepover?" I asked Samatra one day at school.

I had been to her house for a sleepover. It'd been fun. We'd spent the night eating junk food and talking, and now I wanted to return the favor.

She agreed without hesitation, and I was overly excited.

I spent my rides home that week planning my sleepover with Samatra: what we would eat, the games we would play, the stories I would tell, and, of course, introducing her to Cindy and the other girls. I told Dorothy about the sleepover, and she gave me permission. I could tell immediately that she was happy I was having a sleepover with a friend from school, particularly a friend outside our neighborhood.

When the day of the sleepover finally came, I was in a bubble of excitement. And Samatra was, too, when she pulled into my neighborhood in a small car. Someone from home had dropped her off.

I took her up to our apartment to drop her bag, proud to be showing her the three-bedroom Dorothy had rented us. Afterward, I took her around the neighborhood to visit Cindy and the girls. Their eyes widened when they saw Samatra, and I could tell that Cindy was a little jealous. She had always been the one who stood out with her fair skin and now here was Samatra, practically eclipsing her. We played at the playground, talking and laughing hard, so hard. Afterward, we went home and made homemade donuts with canned biscuits and watched TV while we ate them. Dorothy let us have all the banana-flavored taffies we wanted, smiling and complimenting Samatra, peering in every hour to see how and what we were doing.

It unnerved me, this new attentiveness from Dorothy. But it also pleased me because I could tell that she liked Samatra. She liked the look of her, the way she ate her taffies daintily with her mouth closed and folded her legs under her body neatly like a monk. She liked the bow in her hair, too, and how it matched the rest of her outfit.

When we went to sleep that night, I had a smile on my lips. I had a friend. I had a friend that Dorothy liked.

But, when I walked into school on Monday morning, the air was different. I was still visible, but not in the way Samatra saw, in a different, ominous way. People were giggling and pointing…at me. I ignored it and made my way to class, but when I got there, I saw them laughing. It didn't take me long to realize I was the butt of the joke. Because at that moment, someone blurted out, "Rhoda lives in the ghetto!"

My classmates were laughing hysterically and completely stunned and hurt, I looked at Samatra. She was laughing, too. She told them? I thought incredulously. She told them I lived in the ghetto? How could she do that? I thought we were friends.

The mocking laughter of my classmates followed me as I made my way to my seat. I took it and faced the whiteboard stoically. My heart was completely shattered, but I wasn't going to let them see.

Dozens of kids in that school, each one with different insecurities and fears, and I stood out as the girl who lived in the ghetto.

Being a teenager is like walking on hot coal while juggling knives, with someone in the background screaming at you to walk faster because college is around the corner or juggle harder or quicker because real life is around the corner. Yet, you are supposed to look composed while you do this. Even when the coal hurts your leg and you need a break, you are not supposed to take too much of a break because there's all that life waiting for you.

So, these kids who were trying to figure out how to juggle while walking on hot coals took their pain out on me. Turned the attention away from themselves to me. They called me fat, and they made fun of my shoes, my clothes, my hair, and my neighborhood. Rhoda lives in the ghetto. It was hilarious, funny, to them. But to me, it was the worst thing that could happen. I withdrew into myself, wishing I could go back to being invisible. But Samatra had taken that away from me.

By the end of the school term, a mental health form went around, and when I got to the question that asked if I ever thought about harming myself, I ticked yes. The teacher who took back my form looked surprised. Her face said, "What's so awful that you'd want to kill yourself?"

But she didn't ask me. Instead, she took my forms and directed me to follow her to the school library. The school counselor was there 'counseling' kids. When it was my turn, he sat me down and said many things I don't remember. When he finished talking, it was clear he didn't really care that I'd ticked yes. This was just a procedure. He needed to say he had done this. But if he asked me and listened after, I would have said I felt sad, stuck, and undeserving. I didn't look into my future because I was afraid I'd see Dorothy in it. Except it wouldn't be her, it'd be me, stuck and angry like her, always dreaming of things I could never have because I wasn't the type of person who got them.

I never told Dorothy about the form or about Samatra, no matter how much she asked about her.

Chapter 7:
THE BLAID OF DESPERATION

On my 16th birthday, I woke to Dorothy holding a kitchen knife to my throat. It was summer, school was out, my SLATE summer job hadn't started yet and I was looking forward to walking the park with Cindy.

When I woke to that knife at my throat, I remember my eyes blinking in terror as I searched Dorothy's for understanding and explanation. But they had none, and strangely, she didn't look crazy or scared. She looked like she had thought long and hard about what she was doing, and this was the sanest resolution she could find.

For the first time in my sixteen years, I broke our unspoken rule and, in a small, terrified voice, called her, "Momma." She didn't acknowledge that.

"You have until the end of the day to find yourself a job," she said. "Don't come back to this house if you don't."

Still pointing the knife at me, she pulled away and said, "Get up and get dressed."

I sprung from the bed and ran to my closet. While she looked on, I ransacked my closet and shakingly pulled on the first pair of jeans and top I could find. She watched calmly as I did, still holding the knife like an experienced hostage taker. When I was done, she said, "Don't come back here unless you have a job."

Still in shock, I mumbled an incoherent reply.

She lunged the knife at me. "Do you hear me?!"

"Yes!"

"Good," she said and walked out.

I stood in the middle of my room, in the small heap of my scattered clothes, and wept. My chest pounded so hard that I thought it was going to explode. It hurt; it hurt so bad. I wanted to sit on the ground and cry, but the sharp glint of the knife and the look in Dorothy's eyes stopped me. She had looked so calm, so sane, so collected and that scared me more than the knife itself because how was this normal to her? Afraid she'd come back, I grabbed my bag and rushed out of the house.

Outside, the air smelled fresh and light against my skin, but it hurt to breathe it in. I looked over at Momma's door. It was slightly ajar. I considered walking over there and telling her what Dorothy had done but thought better of it. It was morning, and Momma was likely already at work. Also, she had never been able to control Dorothy. No one but Ray had.

Ignoring the happy chatter of our neighborhood kids, I walked purposefully, thinking about where I could apply for a job while wondering who would hire me on short notice.

After Momma pointed a gun at me, I feared her. Even after she came over to apologize, I still couldn't get over the look in her eyes when she pointed the gun—how unsteady she had looked, how slightly unhinged her eyes had been. So, I feared her, not because I thought she would intentionally hurt me, but because I feared she would do it without meaning to.

Now, having Dorothy hold that knife to my throat made me realize how very alike they were. Except, I fully believed Dorothy would hurt me intentionally.

Being sixteen was no different than being fifteen or fourteen. I still took three buses to school and had become even more withdrawn after the incident with Samatra. My classmates had moved on to taunting someone else, but I couldn't move past the fact that they'd taunted me, too. I put up a wall after that to keep anyone else from knowing me too much and to bash myself against it regularly because I was ashamed of being Rhoda, the girl who lived in the ghetto. It made me even more ashamed to think of what my classmates would think if they knew my mother had just held a knife to my throat.

I walked purposefully, and as I did, I wished the SLATE job had started. If it had, I'd be there right now instead of trudging the streets looking for another job. I'd been walking for several minutes before I turned the corner and saw Amighetti's sandwich shop. Smiling with relief, I walked in, headed straight for the counter, and asked for a job application. The lady behind the counter was busy but she distractedly handed me a job application to fill in and went back to her work. I filled it out and asked for the manager. He came, took the application, and said he'd call me when they had an opening.

That wasn't good enough for me, so I hurried out. I couldn't wait for them to have an opening. I needed to find a job today. I tried not to despair as I walked out. Surely, there was someone somewhere who would hire me.

As I walked on, I remembered an incident with Dorothy that shocked me almost as much as this morning. Dorothy had accused me of liking a man she was seeing. His name was Ronald. He was a nice guy from the neighborhood and was younger than her. He came over to the house twice every week to see Dorothy. He was always clean, and his clothes were always finely pressed. He was a much finer and acceptable contrast to Ray. Ray was in prison again, and it looked to me like Dorothy was getting tired of it. She looked more tired than usual.

The day she accused me of wanting Ronald, I came home from school and found her sitting in her favorite chair, tapping her legs. She looked restless. Her hair, which she often painstakingly styled, was uncombed, and her skin looked ashy, like she hadn't bothered to take a shower that day or rub Vaseline. I paused at the door, wondering what the matter was, trying to figure out how to walk past her without disturbing her or calling any attention to myself. But a few feet into the house, she said, "You like him, don't you?"

"Who?"

"Ronald. YOU LIKE HIM?!"

I stood there shaking in complete disbelief. How could I like him? I barely even gave him any thought.

"No, Dorothy," I said. "I don't. How can you say that?"

"I see the way you look at him!"

"I don't!" I said and burst into tears. "I never look at him!"

"Yes, you do," she said, jumping up from her seat and pointing her fingers fiercely at me.

"No, I don't. I don't like him, Dorothy. Honest."

"YES, YOU DO! YES, YOU DO! STOP LYING. YOUR UGLY ASS BETTER STOP LYING!"

I ran into my room and shut the door while she stood outside screaming and cursing at me. I didn't understand it; I couldn't. I never looked at Ronald and the one time he tried to look at me, I averted my eyes. I treated Dorothy's men that way. There were few, but they were a passing presence to me. People who came and went. Dorothy gave them a place in her life every single time, nurturing and feeding them, making them the center of her existence until she got tired, or they got tired and moved on.

Not me. To me, they were nothing.

For several days afterward, she didn't speak to me, barely even looked at me. She walked past me like I wasn't there, punishing me for daring to like a man that she loved.

I thought about it now as I walked, the scene of her accusation playing over and over in my head. She had been so sure, so certain that I liked him. I wondered where that certainty came from. How could she think that?

In later years, I would come to see her irrational accusations for what it was: fear, narcissism, and her undiagnosed bipolar disorder. Her relationship with Ronald was too brief for me to qualify it, but she loved him and, because of that, was terrified of losing him. Her fear mixed with her sickness, the sickness where she created scenarios in her head, scenarios that involved her being hurt or being the victim and then attacking you for it. She had to find an object for her attack, a face, or a person that was responsible for her hurt, and my sisters and I had the misfortune of always being available to receive it. Ronald would die a few months later in a drug deal gone bad. He'd gotten shot while buying or refusing to pay for his drugs. I remember being so shocked at the news. Ronald had seemed so clean-cut, so well put together, it'd been impossible to know he was using drugs. Dorothy had mourned by sinking in deep silence and boycotting his funeral. She didn't love another man after Ronald.

I'd been walking for nearly an hour now, my eyes peeled for 'we are hiring' signs but finding none so far. I was tired and thirsty, and for a second, I wondered if I should go back home to get some water.

In my hurry to leave the house, I'd forgotten to take any money for snacks or water. Shaking the image of me downing a bottle of water, I turned another corner and went to another sandwich shop, Schlotzsky's. The picture of a sandwich on their new billboard made my mouth water. I hurried into the shop and stood for a second to inhale the delicious aroma of an oven-baked sandwich. I would like to work here, I thought. Please let them hire me.

I hurried over to a man at the corner. He had on a Schlotzsky's T-shirt with a tag that said, manager.

"Are you hiring?" I asked.

The manager shook his head. "We don't have any openings," he said.

"Are you sure?" I asked desperately.

The manager sighed tiredly and said, "Hold on." He walked into the back, and I took the time to look around.

It looked like all the kids had the same idea to spend the first day of summer here. There wasn't much to do in Carr Square, and most of our fast-food joints doubled as our hangout or date spots. I realized then that if I got the job, I would occasionally run into kids in my neighborhood. I said a silent prayer that no one from Lutheran North would show up.

The manager came back a few minutes later with a job application. "Here," he said. "Fill this out, leave a number, and we will get back to you."

I dutifully filled out the application and handed it back. "When will you get back to me?" I asked.

"Soon," he said.

"How soon?"

"We don't have an opening right now, but when we do, I'll call you."

I sighed and walked out.

Two months ago, Dorothy got a job at a bank. It surprised me at first that she would want to work in a place so structured and professional. But then every morning, I watched her as she carefully dressed up and how she spent her time preparing her outfits during the weekend. The more I watched, the more I realized it wasn't the job she loved but the part it allowed her to play: a put-together professional with beautiful outfits. Fearing she would get fired in the first couple of weeks, I watched anxiously as she went out and came back every evening. I stopped worrying after the first month, I realized then she was incredibly determined to keep this job, and I loved it for her. I loved the look it gave her, even though I knew that wasn't who she was. Inside, she was a ball of fire and chaos, waiting to explode any time. But every time she put on her work outfit, she turned to water: soothing, warm water on a cold day. I wished that version of her would stay always, I wished it didn't come out only when she put on her work outfits. I wished it were that version of her that woke me up on my sixteenth birthday.

I looked at my wristwatch; the time was 10 a.m. I'd been walking for almost two hours. Across from me was a worn-out, unpainted park bench. I made my way toward it and sat down to catch my breath. I felt the tears sting my eyes. What was wrong with her? Why did her crazy ass have to act so crazy? What if I didn't get a job? Was she really going to put me out of the house? Where in God's name was she expecting me to go? Dorothy had put us out of the house before with little backpacks filled with clothes. I was ten years old the last time, and even though she'd thrown my backpack at me and my sisters and screamed at us not to come back, I knew we could. I knew we could just give her time to calm down and then sneak back into the house when she wasn't looking. But this morning felt different. She had barely screamed, and that had made it worse. I understood her screams, I knew how to navigate them, but the deadly calm with which she'd held that knife to my throat, I didn't know what to do with that.

I sat on that bench for nearly half an hour before I got up. Resolutely, I made my way to several other restaurants and fast-food joints, and all of them gave me the same answer, "fill out this application, and we will get back to you soon." I filled out application after application after application and by late afternoon, my fingers were sore, my head throbbed, and my legs ached.

I had filled over a dozen applications by then.

I came back to the bench and sat down. That's it, I thought. Dorothy is going to put me out. I started to go over places in my head where I could live if she did put me out but the only one that seemed likely was Momma's. Except she had Bill and Uncle Freddie living with her, and there wouldn't be room for me. Then I thought about begging Dorothy. I had filled over a dozen forms today; surely, she could see that I'd tried. Maybe one of them will call me back tomorrow. Couldn't she wait until tomorrow? She had to, I thought, standing up from the chair. God, please let her understand. I took a deep breath and started the walk back home. I was really parched now and desperate for some water. I walked a few minutes, turned the corner, and came face to face with Burger King.

I paused in surprise. How had I not thought of Burger King? My outfit was all sweaty by this time, and I wondered what the manager would say to me. But I shook off the thought and made my way there. The worst he would tell me to do was fill out an application. If he did, it'd make my case with Dorothy stronger. I could tell her I'd completed over a dozen forms and was waiting to get called back. When I got there, the lunch rush was just winding down, and there was soft chatter and music playing over the speaker system. I scanned the restaurant for the manager and caught him as he came out the back. I hurried over immediately. The name tag on his shirt said 'Herb.'

"Excuse me, sir," I asked. "Are you hiring? I'd like to apply for a job?"

He looked at me and smiled. "As a matter of fact, we are."

I almost cried with relief.

"You need a job right now?"

I nodded eagerly.

He handed me an application. I filled it, handed it back, and waited expectantly.

Herb looked it over. "Great. You can start tomorrow.

"Thank you!" I said and walked out.

Tired and drained, I walked home slowly, going through the entire day in my mind, the image of Dorothy with the knife to my neck replaying. How could she do that? When I got home, she was sitting in the living room with a cigarette in her hand.

"Did you get a job?" she asked.

"Yeah."

"Where?"

"Burger King. I start tomorrow."

"Good," she said.

I walked to my room and didn't realize how much my hands were shaking until I closed the door. I realized at that moment that I was terrified of Dorothy. This fear clung to my heart for years, influencing my every choice, ensuring that everything I did, I did to please her.

I would ask, years later, why she did that, why she put a knife to my throat the morning of my birthday. And she would say it was because she needed to scare me straight.

"I didn't want you ending up pregnant. You were rolling with the wrong crowd."

"You could have just told me," I said.

"You were a smart-mouth teenager. I didn't know how to talk to you."

A lot of my memories are remembered differently by Dorothy. I wonder if it's intentional or if that's just how she remembers it. I was never smart-mouthed, and I barely had enough friends to call them a crowd. That knife didn't just terrify me; it lessened me, further shredding my worth into bits and pieces that I would spend years trying to get back.

It introduced another traumatizing moment for me, one I spent years trying to unpack. The more I tried, the more I wondered if she realized what she stole from me by holding that knife to my throat.

Chapter 8:
Sizing Up

It wasn't until I began working at Burger King that I realized everywhere I'd applied for a job was a place that sold food. I enjoyed walking into the Burger King restaurant and loved the smell of chicken, beef, and French fries. I loved being around so much food because it meant I'd never go hungry. It also meant I could take leftovers back home for my sisters and Dorothy every night.

My first week passed in an exhausting and overwhelming blur. I hurried from home to work, anxious about arriving late or getting a query, and when the job at SLATE started a few weeks later, I found myself juggling both jobs. It didn't occur to me to quit either job because I found earning an income from both sides allowed me to cater to more needs for Dorothy and my little sisters.

I found the job at Burger King more demanding. I rushed out more orders than I cared to count while reminding myself to always be patient and courteous to customers. I met neighborhood friends and old classmates who came in to order their meals. Some of them laughed when they saw me, some of them were impressed, the others didn't care. I preferred the ones who didn't. It allowed me to be just another attendant to them instead of Rhoda from the ghetto. I met customers who took forever to make up their minds. They stood before the counter, going back and forth, trying to decide what they wanted in a restaurant that predominantly sold chicken and burgers, forgetting they were keeping you standing, and your legs were hurting, and that there were five other impatient customers waiting. At the end of the day, I walked home with my achy body, and my brain numb from taking and dispensing orders, unable to rest because I had to do it again tomorrow. Every day I arrived home from work, sometimes with leftovers, other times with a check to help cover a house bill, I would look at Dorothy's face and check for pride, but I never saw any. I checked every day for the first month, looking for a smile or a "well done," or anything to say, "I'm sorry for putting that knife to your neck, thank you for helping out." At some point, it began to feel like I'd imagined the knife. Dorothy acted like it never happened.

After my first year at Burger King, Dorothy convinced me to buy a car. Her credit wasn't strong enough to buy one and after years of cosigning cars and apartments for her, Momma refused to cosign again. I didn't think I needed a car at the time, but I felt partially responsible for the way Dorothy's previous car had turned out. I had driven Dorothy to work one day and was on my way back when another car ran into me, completely wrecking the car. The driver was driving the wrong way on a one-way street, but the minute he hit Dorothy's car, came out, and saw the damage he did, he started screaming and cursing, insisting it was my fault. I still don't know how I made it out alive with only a sore neck—Dorothy's car was completely totaled. A few weeks later, Dorothy found out a local Mazda car dealership had a first-time car-buying program for high schoolers. You could purchase a car and pay it off in monthly installments. And because I was holding down two jobs at the time, I was able to get approved to purchase a cute little white Mazda 323.

Owning my first car was a paradox. It was liberating but also constricting. Liberating because I no longer had to catch three buses to get to school, I simply drove there. But constricting because outside of school, I barely drove it. Dorothy treated the car like it was hers while leaving the burden of payment completely on me. Though I made the payment every month, it made me anxious. I worried about defaulting on my payment because it meant they would take my car away, and I would go back to catching three buses. I worried about Dorothy crashing it because she insisted on using it whenever she wanted. I worried about her getting to work because what if I defaulted on a payment and Dorothy no longer had the car to come and go as she needed? That was my major worry, the fact that I would lose the car, and Dorothy would be disappointed in me.

So, no matter what happened, I kept the payment going, even if it meant denying myself some things. But never Dorothy's bills. I feared her too much.

I made friends at work and for the first time, it felt natural. For the first time, I didn't feel like I had to try, like I had to become someone else, or like I had to do anything to impress. To them, I wasn't Rhoda, the girl from the ghetto, or Rhoda, who was too ugly to get a boyfriend. I was simply Rhoda, another kid who worked at Burger King.

Also, they accepted me because though we were different, in some ways, we were also the same.

There was Karen, who was slightly older, smoked cigarettes, and was a teen mom. She brought her son Lil Andre to work sometimes, and we'd play and coo at him. Sometimes, I'd carry and rock him when I saw she was too tired and overwhelmed to be around him. I watched her with him sometimes, how she laughed at his silly baby antics, smelled his neck to get a whiff of his delicious baby smell, blew bubbles in his tummy, or rocked him gently when he was fussy, and I wondered if Dorothy had ever been like that with me. Karen and I became close enough that she came over to spend weekends at my house. Close enough that she would ask me in between puffs of smoke, "Rhoda, why aren't you having sex yet?"

And I'd say, "Girl, if I had sex and got pregnant, Dorothy would kill me."

She never pressured me or mocked me for it. She understood. Being a teenage mother had given her adult wisdom.

There was Paula, who was White and the same age as Dorothy. She had a hardness about her that made me wonder about her life and the people in it. But also, a softness that allowed her to bestow enormous patience on me when I first started working and mixed up my orders. Sometimes, after work, she would take me to bingo or invite me over to her house, and she would sit and tell me stories of her as a much younger woman. She told the stories with sad nostalgia like she was old and could never be anything other than a worker at Burger King ever again. She had a longing in her voice, too, the kind I heard in Momma's voice when she told me her own stories.

The older I got, the more I realized many women, especially Black women, have this longing in their voices, a sadness they seemed to have been born with or somehow had been passed down from mother to mother, the same longing and sadness Momma gave to Dorothy, and Dorothy poured on us.

I realized, too, that not all women are able to get rid of it.

I bonded with these women over terrible customers, low wages, and long hours. They were good women, the best kind of women I met at the time, and the uniqueness and sameness of our lives made us bond and love each other genuinely.

***

As with many people in my neighborhood, in my home, we were more concerned with eating to our fill than eating healthily. So, there I was for the first time with access to food like I hadn't had before, and I ate to my fill and thought nothing of it until I stopped fitting into my clothes. I'd always been a big teenager, so I didn't understand why I suddenly wasn't fitting into my clothes. All I knew was I wasn't anymore, and I needed to get new clothes. But I'd go to the store I always went to for clothes, pick out an outfit in the same aisle and size I always did, and try it on, only to have a pair of jeans unable to go past my lap or a shirt clinging tightly to my frame. I remember crying and leaving the store in frustration because I tried close to a dozen clothes, and none of them fit me. Was it the food? But I ate just like everyone else at work, and they never seemed to gain weight. Particularly Molly, a coworker who remained thin and petite the entire time we worked there.

I stopped shopping for clothes for a while because my usual store no longer had anything in my size and because I was tired of being ashamed by salespeople who fixed me with smothering looks. Depressed and resigned, I stopped going to shop for clothes with my friends or sisters until Paula explained and introduced me to plus-size stores like Lane Bryant. The first time I went to one, I went alone, ashamed to go with anyone who knew me and even more ashamed to be walking into a store for plus-sized people. But then I pulled a dress, tried it on, it fit me, and I almost wept with relief. I would shop for plus-size clothes from there on. I wonder now if that was a good thing because being able to fit into clothes again kept me disillusioned. Perhaps if I hadn't been able to fit into clothes, I would have realized sooner that because of my genetics, I was naturally predisposed to obesity. I found this out a few years later after I gave birth to my first child, and my weight escalated.

Most people are condescending toward obese people. They think of them as gluttons without self-control. 'You can lose weight! All you have to do is eat healthy and hit the gym.' But in truth, many obese people don't have the luxury of eating healthily. They eat what they can, when they can, and are often too tired after a long day's work to hit the gym.

Also, we are taught what to eat based on what we are fed as children, and as a child, I ate what was available, and the available meals weren't always healthy. Therefore, it requires some level of awareness, education, and desire coupled with intentionality to change your eating patterns.

It's also hard to control what your body is naturally predisposed to, especially when you have no idea your body is predisposed to it.

With my weight 'contained,' I focused on working and accepting the fact that working at Burger King had taken me from dependent to breadwinner. At the end of every month, Dorothy would give me a list of bills that needed sorting in the house. Sometimes, she wouldn't give me a list; she'd simply tell me as I came home, swaying in exhaustion.

"The light bill is due."

"Get groceries on your way back tomorrow."

"Your little sisters need new shoes."

But the truth was, even without being told, I immediately adopted the role the moment I began working. I paid for bills without Dorothy asking and willfully bought my sister's clothes and shoes at Christmas. Often, when they came to me because they needed new shoes, new clothes, new books for school, an allowance, hair money, snack money, and anything else they were certain Dorothy would deny, I gave them happily because it was impossible to say no. Because at ages 11, 9, and 7, I didn't want them to have to go without things that other kids took for granted. Also, because I understood needing something at that age and not having it, and because it felt like my very purpose and existence was to take care of Dorothy and my sisters. I never complained. On and on it went until I began to stagger under the responsibility of making straight As and making enough to support Dorothy and my sisters. All I wanted was a break, and on the days I yearned desperately for one, I had to put it out of my mind because I knew I had no one to rely on aside from myself.

The more I worked to earn, the more I became angry at Dorothy, the more I resented her for every job she quit, and every time she made me go over to Momma's to beg her for money.

Still, the more I worked, the more I came to understand and respect her. I began to appreciate the value of money, the value of a dollar when it's taken out of your paycheck, the relief when you walk into a store and the money in your purse is enough to pay for your groceries, being able to buy a snack in school or come home to electricity because you paid for it the day before, and the importance of setting money aside. We often had to go without these things, but there were times when Dorothy held down a job for longer than a couple of months and we were able to have all of it.

I looked at families who never ran out of these things and had respect for the people who went out to make them happen. Working two jobs and going to school at sixteen gave me a sense of self and a feeling of wonder at myself. Though I often felt the weight to the point of it almost paralyzing me, I marveled that I could do it.

Still, there were days when I wanted to curl up in bed and stay there; when I wanted to go out and be just like my friends; when I wanted my only worry to be boys or cute clothes instead of the empty milk carton sitting in the fridge. My life had revolved around a paycheck, and soon I had tied my worth to being able to provide, being able to give my sisters all the things they needed or handle all the bills Dorothy needed me to. I feared being unable to do it, feared that I would be discarded and loved less if I weren't, and feared that Dorothy would put a knife to my neck again. Because of this fear, I put myself on a pedestal; a place where I wasn't allowed to disappoint anyone, especially Dorothy. A place where I met everyone's needs. I was terrified of falling off this pedestal.

***

The summer after I started working at Burger King, Dorothy would again hold a weapon to a person's neck, but this time, she did it for me.

Every day I walked home from work, I would walk past our park, and in it, I would see this man named Chuck, whose real name was Charles. He was somewhat popular around the neighborhood. Chuck smiled like a Cheshire cat and leered at my breasts like he couldn't wait to grab them. Every day when I walked past, he would look at me and say, "I'mma get you, and I'mma put my D-I-C-K in you. You just wait and see."

He spelled the words out like he didn't think I'd be able to figure them out. I was sixteen years old, holding down two jobs and attending a private school. Did he think I couldn't spell it? Every day, I would walk past, and every day, he would say the same thing to me, licking his lips as he did while his friends egged him on with lewd laughter.

I said nothing to him when he said these things. I simply tried to walk faster with my head down. There was no other way home except through the park, so I was forced to take that way.

To stop him from leering at me, I wore bigger sweaters and longer skirts. I didn't smile and I kept my eyes down. Perhaps the less of me he saw, the better. Still, he continued every single day. It became a fun game for him. I could tell he looked forward to it. I could tell he waited at that spot, at that time, just to say those words to me. I considered telling Dorothy, but I didn't. I hated bothering her with things I didn't think she wanted to be bothered with. She only spoke to us to scream or admonish or cuss, or when she needed to have a bill paid, and even if she hadn't, I didn't know how to tell her what Chuck was saying to me.

I wondered, too, if I was overreacting. Was that what girls my age wanted to be said to them? Was I supposed to be flattered, proud that this man was saying this to me? Was I acting too much like a prude, or was this supposed to be normal? I didn't know. I wasn't sure what to think. I just knew I wanted him to stop.

I thought about telling Momma, but I felt ashamed of the thought. Momma always talked about my body whenever I came to visit.

"You are getting too fat, Rhoda! It's all that food you eat. You need to stop! What's a young girl looking like a grown woman for?!"

Whenever Momma said this, I was too hurt to point out that she was just as big as me, if not bigger. So how was I fat and she wasn't?

Chuck carried on with his assault until one day, I was walking home from work, thankful I wouldn't be working the next day but dreading my encounter with Chuck. As expected, he was there with his big stupid smile and his friends grinning behind him, waiting for it. But this time, rather than catcall, he walked up to me, unzipped his trousers, pulled out his penis and thrust it at me. I shrank back in disgust, stumbled, caught myself, and ran home with his laughter and that of his friends ringing behind me. When I got home, I was heaving and crying and out of breath, and Dorothy was sitting in her favorite chair with a cigarette in her hand.

"Girl, what the hell is wrong with you?" she asked.

I tried to speak, but my tears wouldn't let me.

"Speak up!" she snapped.

I wondered for a split second if I should tell her. I wondered what she would think. I decided to go for it.

"It was Chuck," I sobbed. "He put his penis out at me."

That was all Dorothy needed to hear. She went into the kitchen, opened the fridge, took out the ice pick, stomped out her cigarette, and walked quietly out of the house. Afraid of what she was going to do, I followed her.

We walked silently until we got to the park where Chuck and his friends were. He smirked when he saw me, but when he saw the look on Dorothy's face, his smirk dissolved.

Dorothy didn't miss a step. She walked straight to him, grabbed his shirt, pulled out the ice pick, and held it to his throat. A shiver went down my spine. His friends screamed in alarm, and Chuck whimpered, but Dorothy didn't even flinch. She spoke with a calm I'd never heard before. It was chilling, different from the one she'd had when she held the knife to my neck almost a year ago.

"If you ever look at my daughter again," she said, "if you ever talk to her. If you so much as walk the same damn path as her, I will come back here and put this ice pick through your throat. I'll kill you. Do you understand me?"

Chuck nodded, his face gone slack and bloodless. I looked into his eyes—those same eyes that had leered at me for months—and saw naked terror there, his pupils blown wide like those of a trapped animal. All his swagger had evaporated in an instant, leaving behind only the trembling shell of a coward pressed against Dorothy's ice pick.

Dorothy pulled back and without a word to me, walked away. I followed her, struggling to match her pace, stunned at what she'd just done. I'd felt a lot of feelings towards Dorothy: love, anger, resentment, fear, insecurity but in that moment, all I felt was pride. I couldn't believe she had done that for me.

A few years later, we heard Chuck got arrested for molesting a girl much younger than I was.

That summer of Dorothy holding an ice pick to Chuck's throat, threatening him to protect me; it didn't erase the summer when she held a knife to my throat. But in some way, it lessened the weight of it.

She had threatened to kill a man because of me, and of all the summers I had growing up, that one is still one of my favorites.

Chapter 9:
He Had Me at Hello

I met James at a party a year after I graduated high school.

By this time, I had aged out of the summer program and was working solely at Burger King. After years of combining school with work, I wanted to rest, take the summer off, and catch my breath. But my final year in high school had stolen that option from me, along with the option of college.

Dorothy called me into her room to inform me the school wouldn't give me my diploma because she hadn't paid my tuition for the year. She looked utterly distraught, like she had failed at the one thing she'd set out to accomplish. We were both crushed. I stared out the window, the view taking me back to the days as a little child when I'd walk into Dorothy's room and catch her staring out the window at the houses in our neighborhood. Every time I walked in, she'd say,

"I wish we could have a big house with a white picket fence. Wouldn't that be nice?"

I thought that it was one thing not to be able to afford a house but a diploma, I thought I'd be able to get that at least. Then, as if swept by some wave of determination, Dorothy told me not to worry, that she'd find a way to get me that diploma. In the days that followed, she made a payment arrangement with the school, and they agreed to let me have my diploma if she is stuck with it. She did, and I graduated.

However, after barely graduating high school, I realized college was unlikely for me. I knew Dorothy wouldn't be able to afford it, and though, with my grades, I knew I could be eligible for a scholarship, I didn't want to leave Dorothy with the responsibility of raising my sisters by herself. So, I skipped going to college and enrolled in a teaching program at a local university: Harris Stowe State. It made the most sense to me. It was affordable, and at the time, I was certain I wanted to become a teacher. To make my decision easier, I completely distanced myself from the few friends I'd made in high school who were now going off to college. Years later, I ran into one of them, and she screamed in delight and surprise when she saw me.

"Girl! What happened?!" she exclaimed. "You were supposed to be my roommate in college!"

We laughed, and over lunch, I wanted to tell her why. But it didn't matter anymore. I was grown, different, and working at a job that amazed her. Everything worked out, most of it at least.

I was still working at Burger King when I met James. I had a simple routine: go to work, go to my teaching classes in the evening, come back home, and repeat. I rarely went out to clubs or parties, even when my friends asked me to come with them or borrow my car for the trips. Dorothy was still completely against me dating. Sometimes, it seemed like the possibility of my getting pregnant out of wedlock terrified her more than it should . And although I wondered what it would be like to be in a relationship, I was too busy working to find out. So, when Karen invited me to her party to help cook and set up, I agreed but planned to leave as early as I could.

On the day of the party, I arrived wearing jeans and a shirt. I planned to spend all my time in the kitchen, away from the party.

I spent the next two hours making fried chicken. By the time I was done, the party was in full swing, and I decided to go home. I made my way to the living room to get my bag, and Karen's friend, Cajuna, thrust her child into my arms.

"Here, hold Little Tim for me," she said. "I'll be right back." She dashed to the left, and I groaned. Little Tim was fussy, and I began to rock him gently. Soon, he calmed down.

A few minutes later, a big guy with a gentle, friendly smile walked up to us. He was ridiculously cute and tall, with a smile that featured dimples. I looked away from Little Tim's precious face and looked at him. He looked so unbelievably familiar; it felt like I'd met him before. He said hi to me and I nodded and went back to rocking Lil' Tim. All around us, the music was blaring, and people were singing along and dancing. The noise upset Little Tim, and he got even more fussy. Noticing, our new friend stretched out his hand with a smile.

"Can I hold him?" he asked.

I considered it for a moment. "Are you Tim's brother?" I asked.

He chuckled. "It's the face, isn't it?"

I laughed. That was why he looked familiar. Tim was the father of Cajuna's baby. I met him a couple of times. The resemblance was unmistakable. Feeling more at ease, I handed the baby to him, and he began to rock him. I looked on, impressed, as Lil' Tim quieted in his arms. Of course, I thought Lil' Tim was his nephew.

"I'm James," he said, smiling.

I smiled back. "I'm Rhoda."

"So, enjoying the party?"

"It's alright," I said. "But I'm leaving soon. I have work in the morning." Turning, I looked for Cajuna, but she was nowhere in sight.

"Are you good with the baby?" I asked.

"Babies love me," he said with mock pride, and I chuckled. He wasn't lying. Lil' Tim was completely relaxed in his arms.

"Alright then." I looked at my watch. "Cajuna should be back soon to get the baby. Please let her know I had to leave."

"Sure," he said with a warm smile, and I remember thinking that it was a really nice smile. But I went home and put him completely out of my mind.

A few days later, Karen called me.

"Hey Rhoda, remember Tim's brother, James?" she asked.

"Yeah."

"He asked if he could get your number. Should I give it to him?"

Thinking about his smile, I shrugged. "Alright."

※※※

James and I started by talking on the phone for hours. It took me back to that time when I spent hours talking to the boy who would later slam his door in my face and call me ugly. Except this was different. I felt comfortable with James. We talked like we had known each other our whole lives, like we'd been waiting forever to be friends. I chuckled and giggled on the phone, delighted every time he rang me up, content to go to sleep later than usual and wake up groggy.

Dorothy paid attention to this: the way I suddenly smiled easily, the contentment on my face. Anxiously, I waited for her to say something, waited for her to ask me if I was seeing someone, but she didn't, and that lulled me into a false sense of security.

Soon, James and I spent time together in my car and went to fast-food restaurants. He would watch me in awe as I ate or sipped a drink. The first few times, I was self-conscious because I thought he was looking for imperfection. But I looked back into his eyes and saw admiration. He was awed by me and saw me from the inside instead of only judging me on my physical appearance. I'd never had anyone be awed by me before. It was such a validating feeling. It made it much easier to fall in love with him. And that's exactly where I was when Dorothy cornered me one evening as I walked into the house.

"You need to break up with that boy," she ordered.

I looked at her in shock. I hadn't even told her I was dating anyone.

"I will not have you bringing no ugly ass babies in this house," she continued. "You better break up with him, or I'll put you out of this house."

I felt anger course through me. Put me out? The same house where I paid half the rent and the light and water bill? The same house where I bought groceries and school shoes, and Christmas presents?

"I'm not breaking up with him, Dorothy."

"Girl, what you say?"

"I like him. I'm not breaking up with him."

"Oh, so you grown now?"

"Maybe if you met him then…"

"No! You don't need a man stealing your time and crowding your space."

"James is not like that!"

"They all like that! You better break up with him. I'm warning you. Don't make me put you out!"

She stormed into her room, and I stormed into mine. I finally had something, someone that was good for me. I was not giving that up.

And neither was Dorothy. She barraged me, cussed me, yelled at me while the neighbors and my sisters watched. When I wouldn't budge, she began to bad mouth me to my sisters, telling them I was being selfish, I was letting some man steal me from my family.

In all that time, she never asked to see James. Never asked what he was like, where he lived, who he was. Never asked why I was so taken by him, why I was determined to keep him in my life. Every time she attacked me, I would go over to James's and cry, and he would console me, holding me until my sobs subsided. He never said one bad word about Dorothy; all he did was listen. And that made me love him even more.

In later years, I would realize Dorothy did what she did because she was terrified of losing me to someone else. Because she feared new love in my life, her hold over me would subside. I would no longer crave her attention and validation as much. I would no longer be desperate for her love. James loved me without condition or expectation. He loved everything that I was at a time when I didn't think I was anything.

And Dorothy, she saw that before I did, before I understood it. It threatened and scared her, especially because no one had ever loved her like that.

One Sunday morning, as I lay in bed, tired from pulling a double shift at Burger King, Dorothy walked into my room and threw the words at me. "You keep going with that boy even though I've told you not to. Get pregnant and see if I won't put you out."

Shaking with anger, she walked out. As I lay there, I realized my exhaustion came from working more than two shifts. I was tired – tired of having her scream and accuse me. Tired of having her threaten to put me out. Tired of the instability of her moods and seeking the validation she would never give me. I'd skipped going to get the college experience I desired and was working an exhausting job for her, but it was not enough. It was never going to be enough for her.

Slowly, I got up from the bed and began to pack some of my things. Done, I caught a cab and went to James's house. He didn't ask any questions; he simply took my things into the house. I stayed there for two days before his father said, "She can't stay here, James. You need to get her out."

From there, I moved to Momma's house. By this time, she had moved into some newly renovated apartments called Plaza Square. Although it was located near Carr Square, it was a huge step up from living in the projects. The houses and apartments were much nicer.

While chatting one day, she asked, "Rhoda, you really love this boy?"

I nodded with a sad smile. "Yes."

"Then I think y'all should move in together. If y'all really love each other like you say you do, it will work out."

"You think so?" I asked hopefully and Momma nodded.

Relieved to have Momma's support, I went back home the next day to pack the rest of my things. The living room was dark as I walked in. Dorothy had shut all the windows and was sitting in her favorite chair, head down, shaking her leg. I inhaled anxiously and walked determinedly into the room I shared with Rayneika. There, I began to pack the rest of my things, taking only what I needed and leaving the rest for my sisters. They weren't home, and I was grateful for that. It would have been much more complicated to leave. Done packing, I zipped my box and looked around my room for the last time. I'd been so relieved when Dorothy moved us into this three-bedroom apartment because it meant I got to share a room with only one of my sisters. For the first time, I'd had some space to myself, and I'd spent nights writing to myself and God here. I felt tears sting in my eyes. This was not how I wanted to leave. Was I even ready to leave?

Squaring my shoulders, I grabbed my box and walked out. Momma had already cosigned an apartment for James and me in Plaza Square. What was done was done.

Dorothy was still in her chair when I walked out, but she was looking at me now with the saddest expression on her face. My heart skipped when I saw it, and I stalled.

"So, you really leaving?" she asked.

I nodded, and she burst into tears.

Willing myself not to cry, I stood there, torn completely at the thought of abandoning her, wondering if I was doing the right thing. But then, I thought of James and the life I could have outside of this house, and my resolve steeled.

I took a firm hold of my box and walked out.

Chapter 10:
SHACKING UP

I was anxious about moving in with James. Anxious about failing at this thing I desperately wanted to succeed at. Anxious that James would wake up one day and not want me anymore. Anxious that Dorothy was right and that he would leave me the moment I got pregnant. But some of that fear receded when we went to see our new apartment.

It was located about ten minutes from Dorothy. It was nice, modern, clean and had that new house smell. Pride filled me as I looked at it. James and I had paid for this. It was ours. We could do this. Everything would be all right. As if reading my mind, James took my hand and looked at me. "We got this," he said. And I nodded.

On our first night in our new home, James dragged a bed into our bedroom. We didn't have a frame for it yet. So, he set it down on the floor with a big grin on his face and laughing, we made love. As we lay in bed afterward, with our bed just a few inches from the bare floor, I realized in that moment, I'd never felt more seen; more loved.

The next day, James and I went hunting for furniture in the basement of his parents' house. We couldn't get new furniture because they came with price tags we couldn't afford. Between my job and his paycheck as a cleaner in an office building, we were poor.

The landlord wouldn't have let us rent the apartment if Momma hadn't cosigned for us.

James's parents, Mr. and Mrs. Banks, were home when we got there, and they said no word of opposition to us. They gave us free access to their basement and even some food while there. I had assumed James's parents would be opposed to us living together. His Dad was a preacher, and his mother was tall, big-boned, and had an air I found intimidating. But they said nothing as we walked past with their old furniture.

We were able to get an old wooden kitchen table with three chairs and old living room chairs. Later, we bought a set of living room tables from James's cousin for $50. The furniture we got from James's parents was sturdy, but time had stolen their beauty. So, that afternoon, while I stayed home cleaning up the apartment, James went out to get some blue and gold paint. When he came back, he put on some music, passed me a paintbrush, and together, we painted our new, used furniture.

Before moving in with James, quietness was a luxury, something I only got at night when everyone else was asleep. And even then, you didn't have to strain your ears hard to hear the occasional, distant sound of gunshots. Sounds like that used to make me anxious and take me back to when I was five and the bad man shot at us. There were days when I woke up to the sounds of Ray beating on Dorothy. Or Momma and Dorothy screaming at each other, or my sisters running around, playing, and yelling. So, it surprised me when, for the first time, I woke up quiet, cuddled in James's arms. It was peaceful and tranquil and being there by myself on the days when I returned from work before James made it feel like I was meeting myself for the first time. I could hear my thoughts, the soft sounds of my feet as I walked through our apartment, the gentle rustle of clothes as I washed and folded. The soft clink of pans and pots felt too loud sometimes like I was interrupting the silence.

I loved this silence, but I also was afraid of it because my thoughts had gotten louder, and many of them were filled with Dorothy. I liked it better when James was home, and we could enjoy the peace together.

I started learning to cook. Before James, all I really knew how to make were sandwiches. Back home, Dorothy used to make elaborate meals every Sunday, but she just never made time to teach me to cook. I wonder about that now. Cooking together is an intimate thing, something with the power to potentially bond—something that requires patience and encouragement, two things Dorothy didn't know how to give. Still, I never saw Dorothy and Momma cook together, so Dorothy couldn't pass down what she was never shown. I had never thought much about cooking before James, but with him, I was eager to learn. I wanted to fix meals for both of us, I wanted to watch him as he ate it. I loved watching him, seeing the gentle smile on his face or the way his face lit up when he saw me. I loved how kind his features were and how particular he was not to have them angry at me.

When I tried to cook by myself, he would join me, putting this, adding that, or asking how he could help. I was often clueless, so we usually figured it out together, following recipes that worked with very minimal groceries. One night, with our fridge empty of groceries, James and I went out to Union Station to eat lunch at O.T. Hodge, a small restaurant in the food court portion of Union Station. We had no money and decided to pay with the coins we'd been saving up. After we finished our meal, as I watched James painstakingly count each coin, I feared he would have to walk back to the house to get the rest. The server shuffled her feet impatiently, and I smiled at her anxiously, imploring her patience. I felt relieved when the coin reached the amount and smiled heartily as he gave it to the server. Our joint paychecks went to things like rent, groceries, light, and water bills. We were too poor to afford anything else. Anything we couldn't afford or had run out of, we took from James's parents' home: toilet paper, bed sheets, towels, spices, and food. Mrs. Banks loved to shop and often bought things in bulk, so there was always something to take when we came over. I think back now about how supportive they were, even though they likely didn't support our decision to move in together. They were there for us, and as a parent, I've learned it's the one thing you can be for your kids, even when you don't support their decisions.

***

Though I still paid for the car note, I left my car back home for Dorothy as a peace offering. But that didn't stop her from calling to cuss me out or scream at me. The woman who had cried the day I left was gone, and in her place was a raging, furious mother determined to punish me for defying her. I dreaded her calls. They broke into the life I was trying to create for myself, reminding me that Dorothy would always be a part of it. I also dreaded it because I could never say no to her. I'd stay on the phone when she cussed at me, not hanging up until she was done. In some way, I felt like I had abandoned her, so suffering through her calls and abuse was my penance. She told my sisters I'd abandoned them, that I'd become worse than Momma with Bill, shacking up with a man and giving him my money when her family was in need. That hurt worse than anything; to have my sisters think I'd willingly abandon them, to have them think they couldn't count on me anymore. And if I weren't so in love with James and the life we were building together, I would have gone back home just to prove Dorothy wrong.

Every time Dorothy called to abuse me, I would cry afterward and break out in hives. James would come home and find me crying or miserable and then proceed to cheer me up. Even then, he still never said a bad word about Dorothy. Though she didn't deserve it, his love and respect for me extended to her. This love and respect were further tested when Dorothy moved in with us.

Momma came over to the house. I had just got off work and was trying to make dinner. I had finished slicing onions and was about to start on the carrots when I heard her voice. Rather than knock, she yelled my name from outside.

"Rhoda! Come let me in!"

Laughing, I set the knife down and walked to the door.

"Hi, Momma," I said as she walked in. She stood for a moment and took a quick look at our old furniture. James and I had spent time refurbishing them and they looked almost as good as new. I was always particular about keeping it and the house clean and had put a flower vase on the tiny coffee table in the middle of the room.

"Very nice place you have here, Rhoda," she said.

I beamed.

"It's small, but you gon have to make space for your Momma and sisters."

The smile left my face. "What?"

"You know they live in your Momma's car now? All four of them. The landlord kicked them out."

"Since when?"

"Two weeks now."

Dorothy and I used to split the rent when I still lived at home. My moving out had made her unable to keep up. I felt a pang of guilt. She must hate me even more now.

"They can't stay here," I said regretfully. "There won't be enough space for all of us."

"You are going to let your Momma sleep out in the streets?"

I said nothing. I didn't have the guts to remind her that my Momma was her daughter, too. Or that my Momma had kicked me out and didn't care if I slept on the streets. I thought about my sisters out in the car at night. What if they got attacked? Raped? Or caught a stray bullet? Dorothy was crazy, but not enough to protect them from all of that.

Then I thought of Dorothy and her moods, her constant yelling, her selfishness, and the fact that she despised James and had spent the entire time since I moved out cussing us. Why did Momma think she would want to live here in the first place?

"She's got no choice," Momma said.

"I have to ask James," I said. "There's really not enough room."

"She won't stay here for long. It's just until she can get a job and get back on her feet again."

I sighed deeply and nodded.

"Thank you," she said.

I told James when he returned from work, and he agreed. Some part of me had wished he wouldn't, so at least I could use that as an excuse. But James was too kind to turn them down. So, a week later, Dorothy and my sisters moved in, and our peace disappeared.

She walked into our home with my sisters shuffling behind her, and unlike her mother, after scanning it, she turned up her nose and snorted.

"I cannot believe you are over here playing house with this nigga while your sisters and I have been living on the street. You are selfish, Rhoda! Your ugly ass is so selfish!"

I said nothing to that. Instead, I moved the coffee table, laid down a mattress for her and my sisters to sleep on, and ordered pizza because I didn't have enough groceries in the house to make dinner. When James returned, she barely said two words to him, even though he greeted her. My sisters greeted him politely, and when we went to bed that night, I wondered if I had made a terrible mistake.

From that night, Dorothy looked for opportunities to pick fights with James. If he came home a minute later, she would say he was probably with another woman and then snarl at me. "Your ugly ass can't keep a man, Rhoda. I told you."

One time, she walked into our room, saw me on the bed, and said, "Y'all's room is so cold. It's because there's no real love in it."

I cried when she said that one. Because James and I had a fight the night before, and I was scared he wouldn't love me anymore.

Having Dorothy in our home reinforced all my insecurities, all my fears, and anxieties. She would spend all day at home and cuss at me when I returned. She would cuss at James too, screaming at him, telling him she knew he had brainwashed me; he and his damn family had bewitched me.

I started to wish she would get out of the house, get a job, leave, something, anything to keep her out of the house. Her cussing and screaming kept us up at night, but no matter how much she cussed at James, no matter what she said to him, he never responded. He was more focused on making enough for us to eat. Our joint paycheck was barely enough to keep us afloat, and adding Dorothy and my sisters made it worse. I started to break out in hives again, crying myself to sleep at night and wishing she would leave. Then, I began to fear that James would leave. He would have enough of Dorothy's craziness and go back to his sane, Christian family. That fear added to my stress and kept me awake for hours at night, leaving me sleepy and exhausted at work.

I called Momma crying, and though she sympathized, I could always tell she was rolling her eyes in exasperation. She really hated crying. "Give it a few weeks," she said. "She'll be out soon." Then she'd add, "You have to be strong, Rhoda. You can't cry over every little thing she says to you."

Chastised, I would dry my tears and say, "I just want to know when she's leaving, Momma."

"Just give it time," she'd say.

That was the problem. I'd had plenty of time with Dorothy; I didn't want anymore. But I listened to Momma, hoping that something would change, and she would leave. But she didn't until one day.

I came home, and my sisters told me Dorothy held a gun to James's head. I stood there in shock. I didn't have to ask why she did it; I knew. She was jealous and angry that she could no longer control me. Even living with us, she could see I had pulled away from her, and every hurtful word she said only made me increase my distance. She'd thought the mockery and abuse of my relationship with James would pull me back, and when she saw that wasn't working, she resorted to violence.

I felt something in me shift. I didn't ask her what happened. I didn't want to know her side. It was so normal to do that in my family; to point a gun at each other like it was a toy, like it wasn't something that could kill, that could end a life, leaving misery and grief behind. James hadn't told me what happened either, and when I asked him, he shrugged and said, "You know how she is."

That night, I called Momma and told her I was done. She needed to get Dorothy out of my house.

"But Rhoda," she started.

"No. No." I said. "She held a gun to James's head."

And Momma went quiet,

"You know your Momma don't mean nothing by it," she said softly.

"Come get her, Momma. Please."

She came to get her that very night and took them to her house.

After Dorothy left, I called to let her know I would no longer pay the car note. If she wanted to keep driving it, she had to keep up with the payments herself.

She defaulted on it the very next month, and the dealership called me about it. But when I called her about it, she cussed me. She drove the car for months, and each month, the dealership called to remind me about the payments. Eventually, tired of the calls and knowing it would go against my credit but having no choice because I could no longer afford the payments, I gave them Dorothy's address to go repossess the car. And she called in a rage to cuss me some more; called me ugly, called me fat, told me she would stick me with an ice pick when she saw me.

I would curl up in a ball crying, telling James I wanted to die, telling him no one loved me. And he'd remind me he did; he always would. When the threats and the cussing got too much, I called the police to report her, and they asked me:

"Why is your mother doing this to you?"

And crying, I said, "I don't know."

Chapter 11:
Choosing to Create Life

I dreamt of the perfect man, a happy marriage, and a beautiful home, but never kids. I never wanted them. In some way, I'd already been a mom to my little sisters—taking care of their needs, buying their clothes, shoes, and Christmas presents, and protecting them from Dorothy's moods. I already knew what it felt like to worry about having the light or water cut off, not for me but for the people who relied on me. So, I didn't want that responsibility anymore. I didn't want to wake up to screaming kids or be like Dorothy, who sometimes looked at us like she couldn't believe we were there or hers. I didn't want to hide snacks from my kids and scream at them when they took them without permission. I'd always cried when Dorothy did that. The snacks were always hers, never ours.

I didn't want to be like Momma, with a son who used to beat his sister and a daughter who hated her. I didn't want to spend the rest of my life trying to make it up to them like she did with Dorothy, only to have them throw it back in my face. I didn't want to be the mom who screamed at my children, who chose a man over them, who missed all the big moments, who made them beg for her love, who stole their worth and made them feel less and unworthy.

I didn't want to be like my dad because if somehow, I was unable to always be there, then my children would walk around with a giant emptiness in their hearts, wondering if they were ever loved by a mother they never met. Having children felt like an anchor, a trap, a thing that I would fail miserably at. So, I made up my mind early on not to have any. It was better to die childless than to bring into the world a child whose fate you couldn't control.

But James wanted kids. He spoke of them with a light in his eyes that surprised me. He talked about being a father, about taking his son to basketball games or his daughter to the school dance. And especially, he talked about how much he wanted to have kids with me.

James was great with kids. They seemed to love and instinctively gravitate toward him. Perhaps it had to do with his warmth and the fact that he was built like a warm, cuddly bear. Or maybe it was because he knew just the thing to say or do to get a crying kid smiling again. He was great with his nephew Lil' Tim. He was always happy to hold him, watch, and play with him, even calling him by the nickname, Peanut. I watched these interactions with a nagging worry because how do you tell the man that you love, a man this good with kids, that you don't want kids?

One day after dinner, after weeks of Dorothy being gone, after we'd settled into each other, wrapping each other up in a love we couldn't believe we had, James said, "Rhoda, let's have a baby."

My heart skipped in panic. "What?"

"Let's have a baby," he repeated. "Don't you want to be a family?"

I stared at him, thinking as if he traced a finger across my lips ever so gently. He'd used the word family so casually as if he couldn't imagine being anything else with me. Family meant something to him, something beautiful, attainable, and desirable. But for me, except for moments here and there, it'd always be ugly, chaotic, and dysfunctional.

"You really want to be a family?" I asked.

"Why not?" he replied. "We are already living together, and we love each other," he said, nipping at my neck, as I giggled from the pleasure of it. "You would make a great mom, Rhoda. Don't you want that?"

I stared at him again, playing his words over and over in my head. 'You would be a great mom, Rhoda.' He'd said it with certainty as if I was made to be a mother. As if I would excel at the role, as if I'd be the greatest mother there ever was. He had a way of doing that, of looking at me and seeing in myself that I didn't see or couldn't dare accept. He looked at me like I was whole, like there were no parts missing. I don't know how he did it, but there were days I went to sleep thinking he was determined to pick up the shards Dorothy had left behind and make beautiful stained glass out of them.

"I don't know how to be a mother," I said.

"Of course you do," he said.

"What about school?" I asked. I'd been unable to finish my teaching program. Keeping up with payments was harder than I thought. But I still wanted to go to school. I just wasn't sure when, how, or what school.

"We can make it work," James replied. "And I'll help. I'll take care of our baby too. It doesn't have to be now. But I would love to have a kid with you someday." He gave me a kiss and snuggled closer, and a few minutes later, he fell asleep.

But I stayed up and thought about his face and how it lit up every time he played with his nephew. How happy he always was. James was every bit as young as I was, but his soul was old. He talked and worked like a man who had been here before, like he was here to do better, fulfill something he hadn't the first time around. I loved that man. I loved how he loved me, and I wanted to make him happy.

So, although every fiber of my being fought against it. Although I knew I wasn't ready. Although the thought of having a child made me want to find a table and hide under it, I made my decision. I would make a great mom.

"Let's have a kid," I said to him the next morning, and his face lit up. He hugged me, and we started to try right from that moment. It didn't take us long. We were pregnant two months later.

***

The day I found out I was pregnant, after excitedly telling James, the only other person I wanted to tell was Momma. So, a week after we found out, we made our way to Momma's apartment. Dorothy and my sisters had lived with Momma until she cosigned an apartment for Dorothy, but now Momma told me they now live in a shelter. She had said it with disappointment to Dorothy but at me, too, and I'd felt horribly guilty. I knew she was unhappy the arrangement with Dorothy hadn't worked. I could tell every time she brought it up and wanted me to make peace. But every time she said it, the image of Dorothy holding a gun to James's head would float in my mind, and I would clamp down on my guilt.

Dorothy had called me every day after she left to cuss and scream at me. Every day. I didn't know it at the time, but I realize now it was displaced anger. She was blaming me for all that was wrong in her life at that time. She said a lot of targeted, hurtful things when she called, like how fat I was and how when she saw me again, she would stick an ice pick in me. She had said it with so much venom that I'd slammed the phone down and burst into tears. James had found me curled up in a fetal position several hours later. I had no idea how long I stayed there, crouched with the image of Dorothy sticking me with an ice pick floating around in my head. I believed her. I'd seen her hold an ice pick to a man's throat. I still remember her holding a knife to mine. She would do it if she saw me again. I had no reason to doubt her.

Momma was in her apron when James and I showed up. She looked tired, like she'd spent the week doing backbreaking work. I wondered if looking this tired was a default of having kids.

"Rhoda!" she said with a tired smile. "You and your man here to see me."

James chuckled. He liked Momma.

I smiled, too, tentatively. I didn't know how she would react to hearing the news.

"How's Bill?" I asked.

"He's off to work," she said, still smiling. She and Bill had been living together for years and were still not married. It still irked Dorothy.

"I need to tell you something, Momma," I said when she sat down.

"Okay, Rhoda. What is it? You are not pregnant, are you?" she said with a half laugh.

I didn't laugh with her.

She straightened and looked at me curiously, like I had a strange hairstyle she was trying to understand. I squirmed under her gaze, and James held my hand.

"You are pregnant, Rhoda?"

I nodded.

"Why?"

"We are going to have a family," James said, and Momma scoffed.

"Raising a child will not be easy, Rhoda."

"I know, Momma."

"No, you don't. It ain't about being in love or wanting a family, although you have more than most women have: a good man and love. But raising a baby isn't easy. Just look at your Momma. She got four kids from three men, and none of them stuck around."

I thought about how the same could be said for her but said nothing. She had been quite lucky to find Bill.

"We will be fine," James said. "I'll take care of her," he added firmly. "I'm not stepping out on her and my baby. We are in this together."

Momma stared at both of us for a long time until I felt James's squirm next to me. I could tell she had much more to say, but she held her tongue.

"You want this baby, Rhoda?"

Did I? I thought as I nodded eagerly. Did I want this baby?

"We both do," James said.

"Then you all should get married. Y'all want to have a family, then make it a real one. Get married. Go to the court and get married."

I looked at James, and he looked at me. "You want to do this?" he asked.

I nodded.

"Okay, let's do this. Let's get married."

✳✳✳

Telling James's family was much different than mine. Maybe because he had a traditional family, with parents who were very invested in his life. I'd expected yelling and scoffing, but his parents went quiet as if they knew something like this was bound to happen.

After a while, Mrs. Banks spoke first. "Your Daddy is a preacher, James," she said. "What do you think people are going to say when..."

"We are getting married, Ma."

That made her pause. She looked both of us over and said, "That's good. When?"

"We are heading to the courthouse on Friday to get married."

She shook her head firmly. "No. My child isn't getting married in a courthouse. You will have a wedding. Your father can marry you." She turned to look at Mr. Banks. "Right, honey?"

He nodded and spoke for the first time, "Yes. But you are both just kids. Are you sure?" He added softly.

James nodded for both of us.

His father nodded back. "Alright."

Mrs. Banks looked at a picture on the wall. It was a photo of James's brother Tim and Cajuna. "I always thought Cajuna would be my first daughter-in-law," she said quietly, and I looked away so she wouldn't see how much that hurt my feelings.

She shrugged and turned back to us. "They will be fine," she said to Mr. Banks. "We will help."

"We don't want a big wedding, ma," James said. "We can't afford it."

"Don't worry. We will pay for everything. Rhoda, what about your mom? Does she know?"

"My grandmother knows," I said.

"And your mom?"

"I haven't told her yet."

"Well, go on and tell her. We have a wedding to plan."

James's mother began to plan our wedding. There was so much to do but I didn't have to do anything besides show up. She was paying for everything: the venue, the cake, the dresses, the food, and even my baby shower six months later. James and I told her we didn't need much but she ignored us and went right ahead to do what she wanted. I thought I would hate having someone plan one of the biggest days of my life, but I didn't. Her excitement and preparation for it helped reduce Dorothy's glaring absence. By now, I knew Momma had told Dorothy, but I also knew she wouldn't care.

Little doubts and insecurities nibbled at me about the wedding, about the baby, about being a mother, but I hid them by throwing myself into the wedding preparation. I compiled a guest list and saw I barely had anyone to invite. Besides Momma, my sisters, and Dorothy, my friends at Burger King, were the only other people of whom I could think. And my childhood friend, Marnie.

A few weeks before our wedding, Momma called me and asked, "Aren't you going to invite your Momma to your wedding?"

I laughed when she asked that, but then I realized I was actually crying. I was getting married, I was having a baby, and my mother didn't care enough to come, to call, or to celebrate with me.

"Rhoda," Momma asked with both alarm and disgust. "Why are you crying?"

"Why does she hate me, Momma?" I asked. "Why?"

"She doesn't hate you, Rhoda. You know how she gets. Just shake it off."

Dorothy did come to my wedding. I would find out later that she did because Momma and Mrs. Banks went to beg her. And she only agreed after they promised to pay for her hair, make-up, and clothes.

"I'm not coming there looking like I live in a shelter," she'd said.

Mrs. Banks paid, not just for Dorothy's, but for my sister's dresses, shoes, jewelry, and stockings too. Rhoshay was part of my bridesmaid, and James's sister, Lynn, was my maid of honor.

At the wedding, Dorothy sat in the back laughing, and chatting with the other guests, never sparing me a word or glance.

James and I got married in the biggest blizzard St. Louis had ever seen. I flew into a panic, sobbing as I thought we would have to cancel everything, but our guests stayed, and Mr. Banks married us.

As my Uncle Curtis walked me down the aisle, I thought of Dorothy in the back seat, a deep frown on her face, merely here out of obligation and no real love. I thought of Momma and what she said, "Raising a child will not be easy," and my panic returned, tightening my chest, and making it hard to breathe.

But then I looked at James and thought about how he'd cut my hair for our pre-wedding photo because we couldn't afford a hairdresser. He'd done it gently, caressing my neck softly and gently massaging oil into my head when he was done. I thought about the night before, how he'd made dinner and rubbed my feet because they were sore from working all day. I thought about how he brought me food and little trinkets whenever he went to work and how he'd held my hand firmly when we told Momma about the pregnancy.

"I'll take care of her," he'd said. "I'll take care of both of them."

The tightness in my chest loosened, and I knew I couldn't have chosen a better partner to do life with.

At the reception, our guests laughed about how crazy the blizzard had been.

"Y'all don't go separating now," they said. "We braved a blizzard for you. Y'all better stay together."

We did. Thirty-three years later, we are still.

Chapter 12:
A Premature Birth

Our mothers will always have a hold on us that's irrevocable. We are tethered to them, molded by them, validated by them, nurtured or damaged by them, and in many cases, we become them. So, every time I felt my baby kick, every time I heard its little heartbeat, mine skipped in fear because I wondered what kind of mother I'd be to this human who would forever be bonded to me in a way that was irrevocable. But even in that, I couldn't quell the excitement that flowed through me. I was about to become a mother. It was nerve-racking, this feeling. I wavered between fear and excitement, afraid to fall into the wrong one.

James was beyond excited. He had a glow, the kind the pregnant woman is supposed to have and a joy that was indescribable. Every day before he got home from work, he would call me and ask me what I wanted. Every morning before he left, he would ask me how I was doing. He held my hair back while I threw up, rubbed my back and feet while I slept, and made dinner even when he was too tired. He got me everything I was craving, whether it was in the middle of the night or at the crack of dawn. Everything I craved was beef-centered, and everything that was beef-centered was at least fifteen minutes away. So, James would stock up on my cravings, and on the days, we ran out, he would go out sleepy, groggy-eyed, or tired to get them for me.

A PREMATURE BIRTH

He wore his wedding ring with pride, the same way he held my hand whenever we took a walk in the evenings or talked about me to his friends. One day, we went to the doctor's appointment, and while we waited for the doctor to see us, James looked at his finger and realized he'd forgotten his ring. He raced home to get it, panting when he returned but happy that he was wearing it.

"Why didn't you just wait until we got home?" I asked in amusement.

"Because I felt empty without it," he said.

The doctor had looked at us with a warm smile and I realized again how lucky I was to be married to a man who felt incomplete without his wedding ring.

Momma was just as excited for her first great-grandchild and even happier that I had a partner to raise it with. She gave me as many tips as she could and kept her prayer circle busy with prayers for me and the baby.

She came over on weekends to cook for me, and every time she came, she brought something for the baby: a bib I'd used as a child, a bottle, a blanket she'd picked up at the thrift store, tiny little baby shoes for when it was old enough to wear, clothes, diapers, anything she thought we would need. Eventually, she arrived with a crib, a simple, sturdy crib perfect enough to fit into the room with James and me. I wept when I saw it and she rolled her eyes.

"It's just a crib, Rhoda. Can't have your baby sleeping on the floor."

James's mother was just as excited and, like Momma, kept us stocked with so many baby supplies that James and I didn't have to buy anything for months after we had the baby. She also kept us bemused with advice and tips.

"Don't eat too much of that beef, Rhoda. You don't want your baby coming out with a big head."

"Make sure you are drinking enough water, Rhoda. Can't have that baby dehydrated."

"You sing Gospel songs to that baby, Rhoda. It's not too young to know the Lord."

Some of her advice aggravated me, but I knew they came from a place of excitement and worry. We were both so young they worried we wouldn't be able to handle it.

The only person who didn't care was Dorothy. She never called, never visited, completely shut me out after the wedding. Still, I found myself yearning for her and worried for her. But I am especially worried about my sisters. I had made it out, but they were stuck and reliant on her, subject to her whims and temperament, being fed by her lies. She told them the most horrible things about me. She told them I'd been brainwashed to not care about them anymore. And when that didn't work, she told them I was selfish. That I was choosing James and his family over them. Hadn't I kicked them out of the house when they had nowhere to go? Did I care that they lived in a disgusting shelter and had to scrap for meals? I was just as selfish as Momma. Her lies made my sisters hate me, and they rarely called or reached out. Somedays, completely overwhelmed by the thought of her hate and rage, I'd cry. It was a heartbreaking thing to be hated by your mother, for daring to love, for daring to live a life separate from the dismal one she provided.

I decided to take solace in James's family. They were so put together and perfect. I felt so lucky to be a part of them until the cracks in their perfection began to show.

A PREMATURE BIRTH

After James and I got married, I shared a closeness with Mr. Banks, close enough that I called him Dad. This closeness was born from isolation. Every time I went over to the house, Mrs. Banks and James's sister, Lynn, didn't make me feel welcome. I wasn't so sure why, but it didn't help that Earl Jr. was my father. Unlike me, James had a huge and present extended family. There was always a cousin who knew a cousin whose brother, son, or uncle had been killed by Earl Jr.

Whenever I went over, I spent most of my time talking with Mr. Banks. It was through these conversations that I came to know God and form a relationship with Him for myself. All my life, God had felt distant and hidden, even when I wrote letters to Him as a child. But through Mr. Banks, I came to see Him. And not just see Him but see Him in moments of my life I hadn't known He was present. Like the time He saved me from drowning, the car crash in Dorothy's car, and the shoot out when I was five. Moments that seemed random now seemed orchestrated. Like meeting James and even being the daughter of Earl Jr. His benefits paid for my education, an education that exposed me and, in later years, placed me in positions that my ancestors couldn't even dream of. My life changed when I met God. Life stopped happening to me and began to happen for me.

The closeness I shared with Mr. Banks started to bother Mrs. Banks, and before I knew it, I was getting ignored at family gatherings and even when they did speak to me, their words were veiled in spiteful innuendos. Soon, Mrs. Banks was picking apart my flaws and exaggerating my imperfections. I would find out later that someone had started a rumor in the family that I was having an affair with Mr. Banks. James was utterly disgusted and angry when he heard it.

"They think I wouldn't know if my wife and father were having an affair? How dumb is that?"

Dumb, yes, and damaging. It completely ruined my character in the eyes of his extended family. They believed the rumor and treated me accordingly.

This closeness with Mr. Banks brought me one of the best fruits of my life, my faith in God, but it also kept me estranged from my mother-in-law. In time, because of how close Mr. Banks and I got, he would often call me to vent about his and Mrs. Banks's disagreements. I became his go-to to vent about his wife. I'm not sure why he did that, why he chose me, but I was too young to realize how much it undermined Mrs. Banks. Her husband thought he was venting, but in truth, he was dishonoring her. I should never have been privy to their fights and arguments; it was never my place to know. Still, though I never said a bad word about her or disrespected her, she grew resentful and spiteful. Mr. Banks realized what he had done many years later when the damage had been done, when I'd become a pariah in the family.

"I should never have discussed her like that with you," he said. But that brought me little comfort. I did get some from Mrs. Banks years later when she fell sick and apologized to me tenderly.

She said, "You've been a sweet daughter-in-law." "I hope you know I love you."

Her apology warmed my heart, but I still felt the need to say, "I never felt it. I never felt your love."

When she died a week later, I was heartbroken. I knew we would have been so much closer if she hadn't spent all those years hating me.

✳✳✳

A PREMATURE BIRTH

My pregnancy was unusual, and I didn't realize until I was in my seventh month and a robbery occurred in the Barnes Jewish Hospital Garage, where I worked as a cashier attendant. By this time, I had traded my job at Burger King for a daycare job, and now that to become an attendant at the parking garage. It paid more and involved less work. Except for the long hours, the job was mostly easy. I sat in a tiny booth, checked in customers when they parked, calculated their amounts due, and took their payment when they left. I handled a ton of cash daily, and that made me anxious because St. Louis, particularly Carr Square, was known for its drive-by shootings and day-time robberies.

The Friday of the robbery, I sat at my spot going through customer invoices, rubbing my belly, and munching on beef jerky when I heard a woman scream. Alarmed, I dropped the jerky and looked out of my booth. I recognized the woman immediately. She was an employee in the hospital, and she was getting robbed. She screamed again as the thief shoved her to the ground and ran away. My hands shook as I hurriedly dialed 911. The operator picked immediately.

"Hello," I said, "There's a man… there's a robbery. A woman is being robbed."

"Calm down, ma'am," she said. "Where are you?"

My heart pounded, and I clutched it instinctively, "I… uhm… Barnes Jewish Hospital. I'm at the parking garage."

"Alright, stay calm. We are sending help."

After I hung up the call, I waddled over to the woman to help her. She was sobbing, and there was blood on her right cheek from an ugly bite.

"He bit me," she sobbed. "He took my purse. I've got my keys and credit card in there."

I sat with her until the police officers came and realized just how lucky I'd gotten. He could have attacked me, too. It was a wonder he'd gone for her and not for my booth. I had a lot of cash in the drawer.

Shaken and afraid, I called James to take me home. My chest was still pounding as I took my bath that night, but with James rubbing my back, I fell asleep. The next morning, with mild chest pains that I mistook for heartburn, I dressed and went to work. An hour later, I was clutching my chest and struggling to breathe. The pain had worsened. Afraid, I called my doctor, and he instructed me to go to the emergency room. I called James, too, and he arrived at the hospital a few minutes after I did, anxious and beside himself with worry.

The nurse in the emergency room proceeded to check my blood pressure before my doctor arrived.

"Wow!" she exclaimed. "Your blood pressure is way too high."

My doctor, Dr. Murdoch, appeared just then, and that eased some of our worry. We had been coming to this doctor since the conception of our baby. I'd been going to him since I started my period at ten, and he was the doctor who birthed me. I trusted him completely. The nurse relayed my blood pressure to him, and I saw his face cloud with worry.

"How's your urine been looking?" he asked.

I thought for a moment before it hit me. It had been darker than usual for weeks now, but I'd assumed that was just another symptom of being pregnant, like throwing up every single day after breakfast since I conceived.

A PREMATURE BIRTH

"Ma'am?" he asked.

"It's been dark," I said.

"We need to admit you immediately," he said. "If we can't get your blood pressure down, we will have to deliver the baby."

I looked from James to Dr. Murdoch in confusion. What was he talking about? I wasn't due for another two months.

"Doctor," I started, "I don't…"

"Rhoda," he said gently. "I need you to be calm now."

I held James's hand when he said that. There was nothing calm about what he said next.

"You and your baby are in danger. Your blood pressure is too high. I don't think we can help bring it down, and I cannot let you leave here in this state. You could die. We need to get your baby out."

I held James's hand tighter, and Dr. Murdoch continued. "Your baby is premature and may not survive. It's a 50-50 chance. We are doing the operation to save your life. You are the priority."

I clutched my stomach instinctively and shook my head. "No, no," I said. "You can't let my baby die." I turned to James. "Tell them," I said. "Tell him he can't let my baby die."

"It's alright," James said. "Everything will be alright."

Everything seemed to happen quickly then. My head spun as they wheeled me away from James. I looked back at him, and he was standing there looking terrified. I felt dread bubble up with my tears.

"Call Momma!" I called back to James. "Tell her I need her." I kept my hand on my stomach, feeling my baby, willing it to be alright. They couldn't let it die. They couldn't. I wouldn't let them. Somehow, I went from not wanting kids to having this baby I hadn't seen be the center of my life. I'd felt it every single day since I conceived. I'd spoken to it and prayed over it. I felt like I already knew it, like I'd been waiting for it all my life. They couldn't make me a priority. My baby was a priority. It was the only thing that mattered. God, please, I begged. Don't let my baby die.

James called Momma, his mother, and his aunts and an hour later, they had a prayer chain going for me on the phone. Momma came immediately, and her presence calmed me.

"You gon be fine," she said. "It's not your time. You hear me. It's not your time."

I nodded tearfully and rested my head on her bosom. Thrice in my life, I'd almost died, and some part of me had wished that I did. But now, after meeting James, after getting a glimpse of what my life could be with me, after having him love me so tenderly; after feeling my baby inside of me for months, death terrified me. I couldn't leave them behind. I didn't want to go. I wasn't ready to go. So, I prayed harder than I ever had in my whole life. I prayed for my baby, for its little fragile body. I prayed for myself, for the strength to pull through. I want to live, God, I begged. I want my baby to live. Please don't let us die. But, if anyone has to, let it not be my child.

"Want me to call Dorothy?" Momma asked a few hours before the operation.

I nodded. I desperately wanted to hear her voice. I wanted her to tell me I'd be all right. That I'd be fine. That she'd been scared too when she had me, but here I was, alive and well. She hadn't spoken to me since the wedding, but I thought: this is different. She has to speak to you now. She will speak to you. You could die, and no matter how much she hates you; she doesn't want you to die.

Momma called Dorothy right in front of me and told her everything that was happening, and through the awful static, I heard Dorothy say, "So what? I'm not interested in Rhoda right now."

I saw Momma's face change when she said it. I saw her try to mask her emotions so I wouldn't know. The tears were already slipping down my face before she turned. When her eyes locked with mine, she knew that I knew what Dorothy had said. Still, she said, "Sorry, Rhoda. Dorothy can't make it."

That made me cry even harder. Because I could see she was trying to protect me. She didn't want me to know my mother hated me that much.

The operation happened an hour later; I made it out. And so did my son, James Junior, after spending the first month of his life in the Pediatric ICU.

I look back at that surgery now and know I survived because God wanted me to. I know Lil' James made it out, spending a month in the Pediatric ICU instead of two because God wanted him to. But I didn't know his birth would signify the beginning of his troubles. Only God knew that.

Part 2 :
TURNING PAIN INTO POWER

Chapter 13:
THE STRENGTH TO STAND

After the birth of Lil' James, I spent three months partially blind. All I could see were blotches of dark spots. It was scary those first few weeks, worrying if I were going permanently blind, especially after the doctors said they were hopeful my sight would return. I didn't want 'hopeful.' I wanted certainty. They were certain, however, that the partial blindness was a result of toxemia and my blood pressure being so high.

I stayed hopeful while thinking how cruel it would be to never see the face of the child I'd risked my life bringing into the world.

Still partially blind, I spent months making trips to the hospital to get my blood pressure back down to normal, and as it did, my vision got clearer and clearer. When I finally saw Lil' James clearly for the first time—he was the most beautiful sight.

Before that, when I got home that first day without Lil' James, I felt empty. My very essence felt unsteady, incomplete like I had left a piece of me back at the hospital. I was advised to rest, to take the day easy, to eat but I couldn't. I stayed up at night thinking of Lil' James, wondering if he would make it, wondering if James and I had done the right thing by having a child.

'Raising a baby isn't going to be easy, Rhoda,' Momma had said, and I had failed at the first basic task: birthing the baby. In the mornings, I cried as I felt my way around our tiny apartment. It felt bigger now, as if the walls had morphed into a huge, unrecognizable monstrosity just to haunt me. Yet smaller because I couldn't stop bumping into things.

Soon, I dreaded waking up because the mornings were no different from the night. It was dark wherever I turned, so what was the point? I stayed in bed longer, feeling for the trays of food James brought only to push them away.

"You have to eat," James would say, his tone warring between compassion and frustration. "You have to eat so you can be strong when the baby comes."

"And if he doesn't? What if he doesn't make it?"

"He will," James would say. "He will. You'll see. He will come home."

To pacify him, I'd take a bite or two, only to pull the covers up over my eyes, drowning in even more darkness. My strength and mind came back after my baby came home. After I held him, felt his soft, warm skin against mine and knew with certainty that he was all right.

Lil' James was a miracle to me. His birth, his very life. I hold on to that now— when the despair of his current reality hits me now, I hold on to that. There's a purpose, a reason for his birth, and I'll keep holding on to that.

✻✻✻

I thought being a mother would be terrifying, and it was, but from the moment I looked into Lil' James's eyes, all I felt was an indescribable honor that God had put me in charge of someone else's life. Little James clung to me, crying every time I put him down as if he were scared I would never pick him up again, crying when someone else carried him and settling when he was finally in my arms. I clung to him, too, basking in his pure love, worrying when too many hands touched him, and even worrying when people didn't offer to carry him because my son was precious. Why wouldn't they want to hold him? I cried when he cried, frustrated because I didn't know how to make him stop. I sang to him at night because I wanted my voice to be the last thing he heard when he went to sleep. I often wondered, as I held him, if Dorothy's heart had filled with love the way mine did every time I looked at Lil' James. If her heart skipped like mine did when Lil' James smiled. If she cried at my first sit up, first crawl, first step. I wondered if she had ever gone to sleep like I did, with a vow to protect Lil' James from everything bad in the world. I wondered, too, if she had loved me more than she loved herself because I loved Lil' James more than all the world put together.

It wasn't sufficient to say that I loved him to the moon and back because that distance didn't quantify and because I didn't ever want to imagine being that far away from him.

Mrs. Banks fawned over Lil' James, and he basked in it. Every time we were over at their house, Lil' James followed her, crawling behind her and then walking. When he learned how to talk, he began to call her 'honey' because he'd heard his grandparents call each other that. Mrs. Banks laughed in delight every time he did this and popped a candy in his mouth.

"You've got a precious little boy, Rhoda," she would say. "Just precious!"

I loved how happy Lil' James was whenever he was with them or with Momma. As if he knew he was loved and had been fully wanted. It was a feeling I'd struggled for years to experience and to see it radiate out of my son made me believe even more in God.

Having Momma live in the same building was beyond convenient. She came around as often as she could, buying things for Lil' James and playing with him. She was there when we ran out of money to buy food or diapers for Lil' James, giving us money and shushing us before we could thank her. She took Lil' James whenever I had to work longer at the parking garage, spending hours with him. He made her happy, I could tell. Lil' James had a smile and a spirit that could thaw any heart. He waddled to her every time she came, giggling in delight every time she picked him up and spun him. I would watch them happily, thankful that Lil' James had Momma's love in a way I hadn't. Momma seemed softer with Lil' James. She didn't get aggravated when he cried or snap at him to get stronger. She was different with him, even patting him and doing her best to soothe him when he cried.

It helped that Lil' James was a happy, mischievous child who rarely cried.

Momma was married to Bill now, but the certificate was just a formality. They had been married in ways no document could fully capture. She and Bill had been together since I was a little girl, and I was so impressed at how long they had lasted. It made me happy to have such stability in my family. It made Momma happy to be married to Bill, I could tell. She had a partner who supported her and took care of her. I was thankful she wasn't doing life alone.

Momma's happiness and marriage to Bill poured into her general outlook on life, and she went around trying to fix our family, begging me to reach out to Dorothy to make peace with her. She wanted us to be as happy as she was. I could see she wanted us to become a big happy family, the one we would be if we weren't all separated by years of trauma and repressed emotions.

Her badgering worked because the more I bonded with Lil' James, the more I thought about Dorothy. She still wasn't speaking to me, not even after the hospital and the blindness. It puzzled me sometimes, and other times it broke my heart. I thought about giving up on her, moving on, but I constantly felt myself pulled toward her, and the more I experienced this, the more I realized I didn't want this pull to break. I wanted my mother to be in my life, I wanted her to meet my son who, when he squinted, looked just like her. I wanted her to be a normal mother, to come over and berate me because I forgot to put socks on Lil' James's feet. But on the other hand, I wanted her to stay far away from me, to never meet Lil' James so she wouldn't steal his essence like she tried to do mine.

"She's your Momma, Rhoda," Momma would say every time she came to visit. "Try and make up with her. It's what God would want."

"She's the one who doesn't want to see us," I would reply. "She's the one who wouldn't come to the hospital to see me."

"You know how your Momma can be. But that doesn't mean you gotta be like that. She could walk past Lil' James and not know him. That ain't right."

I laughed at that.

"I don't know, Momma. I don't really think she wants to see me."

"Then you go see her. Take Lil' James with you. That baby is too cute to resist."

But I didn't go, not because I didn't want to but because I didn't know how to reach out. I often wondered what I would say when I saw her or what she would say when she saw me. I wondered how she would have felt if I had died in the hospital and those had been her last words about me. I wondered if she was sorry and if she thought about me as much as I thought about her. I thought about that day she cried when I walked out of the house. I wondered if she would ever forgive me for leaving. But I knew even if she didn't, I would do it all over again.

Eventually, and I'm not sure who called first, we started talking on the phone. There was no shouting or cussing from her; it was mostly civil. She would ask about me and Lil' James, and even James and I'd ask about her and my sisters. She was working now, and they were all right, she would say. I could always hear the unspoken "no thanks to you" at the end of her sentence, but I never commented on it. We left many things unspoken, as if we knew how very fragile the connection was.

But we were speaking again, and for Momma, that was better than nothing.

***

With Lil' James in my life, I focused on being a good mother and even more on bettering myself. It helped that I had a husband who absolutely adored his son and couldn't bear to be apart from him. It became a running joke in our family; you couldn't see Big James without Lil' James. James took him everywhere he went, carefully hoisting him on his shoulder while Lil' James laughed and pointed at everything. He spent all his free time with him, which was a lot because he worked at night as a Janitor while I still worked during the day as the Cashier attendant at the Barnes Jewish Hospital Garage. He kissed Lil' James a lot on the forehead, so much that it became their thing. Lil' James wouldn't let his father leave the house until his father did that, and he wouldn't go to sleep without his forehead kiss, too. All my life, I'd grown up around fathers who were absent or abusive, fathers who never had fathers and so didn't know how to be fathers themselves. Or fathers like mine who were murderers. Or fathers like Ray, who beat their women. So, seeing James be a real father to Lil' James, be the father I'd always wanted for myself, was like a dream, the kind you wake up from thinking could never happen. I loved him even more because he made me believe in fathers again.

While James shined at fatherhood, I learned earnestly how to be a good mother and wife. I called to mind everything I knew about being a mother, but my memory was filled with Dorothy and Momma. Dorothy had never learned to be a mother because Momma hadn't always been a good one to her. She cringed in shame every time she talked about Momma's drinking. How she would be passed out on the street drunk with her skirt riding up while the other children pointed and laughed. How she left them without food or clean clothes. How she didn't do anything when Curtis attacked and beat her. Although Momma became more of a mother to me than Dorothy ever was, the image of her pointing a gun at me never left my mind. I loved her fiercely because she loved me in her own way, often from a place of penance. But I didn't want to be the mother that she was.

So, I learned, in my own way, from a place of fear and determination. What does a mother do? A mother loves, a mother protects, a mother provides. I thought of the many months my sisters and I had to go without necessities because Dorothy couldn't afford it or how she sicced us on Momma to beg for money. Or how she quit job after job, sitting on the couch sometimes for months without working, and I swore to be different.

I worked at the Parking Garage harder than anyone they had ever employed before me. Made sure to get to work early, made sure every dollar was accounted for, and made sure to smile and be polite to the customers even when they were rude to me. I never wanted a reason to tell Lil' James we couldn't afford the things he needed. My little, mischievous boy who never asked for much, who had the warmest, most beautiful smile and hugged me fiercely when I gave him things other kids took for granted. I never wanted that smile to dim, those hugs to slack. I wanted to give him everything I never got the chance to have. So, I worked harder and harder until I got noticed and promoted to Telephone Operator in the Hospital. I saw then that hard work was and could be rewarded, and that bolstered my determination. I worked my way up from there to another promotion as a Patient Account Customer Service representative in the billing office. My growth would follow a long and unbelievable trajectory and there are days when I cannot help but pause and wonder at how I went from Cashier in the Parking garage to Executive Head of Culture and Inclusion in American, AG Credit. But that's a story for another day.

At the time, every promotion meant more money, even if it was just a little bit more. It meant we'd always have groceries, and Lil' James would always have clean new clothes. With every promotion, James and I would celebrate by going out to dinner or buying something we'd been wanting to buy but couldn't afford.

But it worried me that while I climbed and got promoted, James remained working as a night janitor. I wanted him to do more and be more, and I often feared that he didn't believe he had more to offer or could climb the ladder like I was. James was a shy person. A man of few words who really wouldn't speak to you unless you offered or had become familiar to him. I found that part of him endearing at the beginning of our relationship, but now I feared it would limit him.

The harder I worked, the more I got noticed by the bosses and my co-workers at Barnes Jewish Hospital Garage. Every praise and recognition I got from the bosses spurned a jealous remark from my co-workers, particularly the females. They would say hateful things to me to trigger the many insecurities I dealt with internally. I cried when they did this because it was just like being in high school all over again. Until a supervisor called me into her office one day and said to me, "Don't pay attention to these girls. You have the potential to make a lot of money. Focus on that. You need to grow a tough skin."

I listened to her and focused until James, and I saved enough to buy our first house. Lil' James was five years old at the time. When we first realized that we had enough money to purchase a house, it was surreal. We had been saving and setting money aside and when it was finally enough, James and I looked at our balance as if we couldn't believe it. Excited and cautious at our good fortune, we carefully and meticulously shopped for the perfect house, and when we finally found it, I called Dorothy in excitement.

"Are you serious?!" she asked.

"Yes!" I said, laughing. "It's a two-bedroom with a bath and a small basement. Do you want to come see it?"

She did. James and I brought her over to see it the day we were handed our keys. She was the first of our extended family to see it. That was the first time I had seen her in five years. I was a little anxious about seeing her, but when I did, the years dissolved, and though I was a mother now, it still felt like I was the 19-year-old Rhoda walking out of her house for the last time. She didn't give any indication that she was anxious about the meeting. She was the same old Dorothy. She looked well, barely looking older than the last time I saw her, and I was thankful for that.

I brought her into the house and took her around, and her eyes shone with a mixture of surprise and shock. Our new house looked just like houses she'd wished she could buy us when I was a child. As she looked around, I thought about how much Dorothy loved and always wanted fine things but just hadn't known how to get them. I wondered, too, if living in a house with a white picket fence would have made her a better mom.

"I didn't believe you were really going to buy a house," she said. "But you did it!"

I laughed at the awe and surprise in her voice, completely delighted by it. She went through the house, checking this and that, and for a moment, I felt guilty that I'd bought the white picket fence house before she did. But she looked genuinely happy for me, and I relaxed.

"You are going to host everything now," she said. "The 4th of July, Christmas, and Thanksgiving. Everybody can come!"

"Of course, Dorothy," I'd said, laughing. "Especially you."

Buying that house made James and I work even harder. We have a mortgage added to our responsibilities now. I doubled my efforts at work to get noticed, and one day, my supervisor called me to her office.

"Have you ever thought about going to college?"

I thought about my teaching course and sighed. I barely kept up with my classes.

"I don't think I can," I said to her. "I don't have the time, and I really can't afford it."

"I think you should. You are smart and hardworking, and having a college degree will open more doors for you."

I thought about it all the way home and brought it up with James a week later.

"I've always wanted to go," I said. "And this will open more doors for me. I can earn more. It will be good for us. For our family."

James looked at me for a long time, and just as I feared he would say no, he said, "You should go. Don't worry about Lil' James. I work nights. I'll take care of him when you are in class."

I hugged him tightly and he laughed as he hugged me back. Lil' James stood beside us, jumping, trying to get into the hug, and James lifted him up so he could. Later that night, he asked me, "What course are you going to study?"

"Business Administration," I said. It made the most sense to me. I wanted something that I could apply in any industry.

A few weeks later, I registered for classes and learned I had to buy books for my first class. The books were expensive and way out of my budget. So, I told the school I would return after I'd saved enough to afford my books.

My supervisor followed up with me a couple of weeks later to find out how my classes were going, and I sadly told her they weren't.

"'I've registered," I said. "But I will have to wait because I can't afford the books."

And with a smile, she wrote a check for me. "College books are very expensive," she said. "But this should help."

Too stunned to speak, my eyes watered, and I swore at that moment to make her proud. It was strange to have this woman believe in me so much. So much so that during summer, she would send boxes of toys and learning activities for Lil' James to keep him busy while I studied.

I looked for her after I graduated college with honors, an honor I didn't even know about until the graduation ceremony rehearsal. I walked into the hall with a white rope on my gown, and one of my classmates exclaimed in shock and delight.

"Congratulations, Rhoda!"

"For what?" I replied in confusion.

"You are graduating with honors!" another one said. "That's why you have that white rope on your gown!"

"Wow! I had no idea!"

Turns out I'd graduated cum laude. I realized later I would have graduated Summa Cum Laude had the teacher not given me a C in my first class.

I'd be so busy putting in the hours and doing the work to check my grades. When I found out my hard work had resulted in honors, all I wanted to do was run to my supervisor, the woman who paid for my first set of college books, and say, see! Look what you made happen! But she had relocated to Texas by then, so I had to settle for a phone call.

It was uphill from there. I got promoted to supervisor and then took another job as an analyst. It was happening; I was growing, becoming, and doing the thing the women before me hadn't been able to do. I was making more money, and I was happy. I had a great husband and an amazing son.

But life is never without chaos, hurt, or pain, and I'd foolishly thought I was due for a break. But everything else I'd been through paled in comparison to what came after.

And it did in the form of Lil' James.

Chapter 14:
The Other Side of Dorothy

When I was pregnant with Lil' James, I used to jokingly say to Mrs. Banks, "I hope I have a bad little boy." We would laugh about it, and then she would say, jokingly too, "Be careful what you wish for, Rhoda."

But Lil' James was a typical little boy, albeit more mischievous. As a toddler, he was the only grandchild who cutely called his grandmother 'honey,' but he could also be very sneaky. He would take stuff, hide it, and then lie about it, and he would play pranks on little boys his age. But he was outgoing, helpful, and had the cutest smile. So, there was no sign, nothing to indicate my cute, outgoing, mischievous little boy would someday become a man I wouldn't recognize.

One day, the sound of a firecracker pulled me from our bedroom into the living room. I walked in to find smoke rising from the middle of the living room carpet. Alarmed, I rushed to it and found a burned hole in the carpet. Someone had lit a firecracker in the living room.

"James!" I called. "Come see this!"

James came over, bent, and examined the hole. "Someone lit a firecracker in the living room?" he asked in surprise. We looked at each other and knew only one person could have done it.

When we called Lil' James, he walked into the living room with his most innocent look, and I knew immediately he had lit the firecracker. He was seven years old then, taller, and bigger than every kid his age, just as I had been at his age.

"Why did you do this?!" I yelled. "You burned a hole in the carpet."

He got immediately defensive. "I didn't do it, Mom."

"Now, don't lie," James said a little more calmly. "We know it was you."

"It wasn't me," he insisted, fidgeting anxiously.

"James!" I snapped

"I didn't do it!"

"Calm down, Rhoda," his dad said. I did, but I was terribly upset because he was lying about it. There were only three of us in the house. Who was he trying to pass it off to? Also, the switch in his look surprised me. He was looking at me defiantly now. He had looked so innocent a few minutes ago.

"We just want to know who did it," I said. "You won't get into any trouble."

"I didn't do it, Mom."

"It's only three of us in the house," James said. "It wasn't me or your Momma. "If you didn't do it, who did?"

"Maybe someone from outside did it," Lil' James said.

"Which someone?"

"I don't know! Someone."

"Someone?"

"Yeah, someone."

We asked him some more, and he insisted it wasn't him. The more we asked him, the angrier he got until James, angry now, sent him to his room.

That night, I pondered it. He had seemed so insistent, hurt, and angry that we had even suspected him. Maybe he hadn't lit the firecracker. I said the same to James as he got into bed.

"He did," James said without missing a beat. "We have to be firmer with him. You saw how angry he got when we questioned him? He's got a fiery temper. We have to be firmer with him."

I went to bed that night, thinking of someone else I knew who had a fiery temper.

***

Our new home brought a side of Dorothy I didn't know existed: the fun grandma. Once we settled in, she came to visit as much as she could. When she did, she would play games with Lil' James, games where they were laughing happily and having fun. It surprised me when I witnessed it because I never thought Dorothy could be the grandmother who would sit on the floor with her grandson and play firefighter truck games with him. She even had a better relationship with James. Some weekends, they would sit outside barbecuing and would play cards and dominos. I'd look at them and remember that once she held a gun to his head and wonder how they had made it from that to this. It helped that James was forgiving, that he was intentional about not holding any grudges against her.

Our relationship improved, too, because neither of us ventured into the past. I never confronted her about not coming to see me in the hospital or the five years when she had deliberately iced me out of her life. We got along surprisingly well. I would go over to her place on some weekends, taking Lil' James with me, and she would come over to ours. She laughed more during this period, and more importantly, she laughed with me. I loved that. I loved meeting this Dorothy, the one happy to spend time with me and her grandchild.

The closer we got, the more I wondered if she was proud of me. Proud of the fact I'd gone to college and graduated with honors, proud of the fact I was shooting for a Master's now in Human Resources Training and Development. Proud of how far I had come, how much I was making now, and the home I'd made. But she never said anything to me about it. Though, sometimes, I'd catch her looking at me with something akin to jealousy in her eyes. Sometimes, it was awe, and other times it was anger. I never knew why; I never asked. Things were going fine. Our family was functional, together in some sense. No one was hating anyone, at least not openly. Momma was, in a way, having the family she'd always wanted, and I didn't want to rock the boat.

Our house became the designated spot for every celebration: Thanksgiving, Christmas, New Year's, and Fourth of July. I became the overwhelmed host. I would spend days preparing and hours cooking, and everyone would show up, eat, and have fun. It was nice, but it was also exhausting. Just once, I wanted to be invited to someone else's home for the holidays, but when I complained, Dorothy said, "You the one with the house. What do you expect?"

Our home also became the designated spot for squabbles and intense arguments during the holidays, often between Dorothy and Momma. Although it was more of Momma saying literally anything and Dorothy shutting her up. She delighted in making everything Momma said sound dumb and got even more joy from doing it in front of us or Bill. We learned never to get in the middle; we just paused and waited it out.

Every time she did that, I saw that Dorothy was waiting to get some kind of apology from Momma but never got it. She'd been waiting all her life, and her attacks were her way of demanding one.

Still, my relationship with Dorothy and even my sisters was good during that time. Rhoshay and I had gotten closer. We spent time hanging out, sometimes talking about how we survived Dorothy.

Life wasn't perfect, but things were good. Still, sometimes I got the feeling that we were all faking, each one playing the part to keep up the ruse of a big, happy family.

✱✱✱

After Lil' James was born, after the trauma of the operation and the resulting blindness, the doctors were certain we wouldn't have any more children. "We advise that you don't try to have anymore," they had said. They didn't have to tell me twice. I had no intention of having another one. The trauma of the first one still hovered in my mind. So unlike Lil' James, Jaylen wasn't planned. His conception came on the heels of a death, Bill's.

Three years back, Bill was diagnosed with bone cancer. I could tell it was a shock to both him and Momma, but they bore it stoically, never showing fear or anger around us. Bill went back to his normal activities, and for the most part, he was fine until the last six months of his life. His health deteriorated very quickly, and Momma focused her full attention on caring for him and making him as comfortable as possible.

The day before Bill died, I went to their home to stay with Momma because I didn't want her to be alone. Bill was the only man I had known Momma with, the only one who made her smile, and one she had told me loved her and gave her life meaning. Momma never talked about the men before Bill. In many ways, Bill was for Momma what James was for me, and it hurt to see him go.

I stayed with Momma all day, watching her tend to Bill on the hospital bed she had installed for him in their livingroom. I had never seen any affection between Momma and Bill, yet her gentle tending of him was such a raw display of love and affection. It was beautiful to see. Fighting cramps and fully aware my period was coming, I kept going to the bathroom to check, but all I saw was spotting. After the third check, I came back and sat with Momma. There was no doubt now it was almost time; Bill was leaving. I watched Momma watch his face as he took his last breath. She held his hand as he did, as if she wanted him to take her love with him. Afterward, I expected her to cry, but she didn't. She stood up very gently, kissed his forehead, covered him up, and went to call the hospital. After they came to take his body away from the home she and Bill had shared for years, the look in her eyes broke my heart. She'd looked lost, like she didn't know where she was, and worse, she couldn't believe she was there alone.

"Go be with your family," she said to me afterward. She said it firmly, urging me on as if she suddenly saw how precious our time with them was. But I couldn't bring myself to leave because I didn't want her to be alone that day.

On my way home the next day, I stopped by the pharmacy to purchase three pregnancy tests. My period still hadn't come, and the spotting was making me suspicious in a scary way. My period was always on the clock. I had never had to worry or fret about it. So, it alarmed me that I'd picked up a test to confirm something I hoped wasn't true. It worried me that I was about to pee on a stick when I should have been wearing a pad. But I tried to calm my anxiety. There was no way I was pregnant; it was probably stress.

Safely home, I went to the bathroom and peed on the first stick; it showed positive. I shook my head disbelievingly, drank a glass of water, waited on edge for several minutes, ripped open the second one, and peed on it. It showed positive. As did the third. I sat on the toilet seat, shaking my head in confusion and doing my best not to panic. We had never used any form of birth control or protection, and after years of not getting pregnant, we were so sure we wouldn't. My mind raced. What did this mean? Could my body carry another baby?

When James got home, I waited for him to ask about Momma and Bill, and then I showed him the tests.

"I think I'm pregnant," I said.

Slowly, he took the tests, sat on our bed, and looked at them in puzzlement. He remained silent for almost a minute before he said, "But after Lil James, the doctor… I didn't think you could get pregnant again."

"I know!" I said, plopping down next to him. "I know," I said more softly. We sat like that for several minutes, just staring until James said. "I think you should go to the doctor."

I was still spotting the next day, so I went to the doctor. I had a different doctor now, recommended to me by a friend. My old doctor had retired. My new doctor was female, Black, and from Jamaica. However, she had traveled. I met an ER nurse who confirmed I was pregnant but didn't understand why I was bleeding. Every perplexed shake of her head increased my anxiety.

"I can see the soft tissue that's causing the bleed," she said, "but I don't know why."

She left to consult with a doctor, and he advised me to go to the emergency room. I sat in that crowded emergency room, trying not to worry. I was certain I would never get pregnant again, and the news of this pregnancy still had me shell-shocked. But the thought of losing this baby, this pregnancy I was slowly beginning to think of as a miracle, terrified me. What if I lost the baby? What if right now I was in danger of losing it?

In need of comfort and not wanting to alarm James, I called Dorothy, and together, we both waited in the emergency room for twelve hours. Eventually, they called me back to a room, and a group of three White male physicians, one of them a resident, examined me and confirmed on the spot that I was having a miscarriage. My breath caught horribly in my chest.

"She's not going to carry this baby to term," he said in the most absolute tone.

I began to cry, and Dorothy stood there, unsure of what to do. One of the doctors decided to call my primary doctor, and when she heard their diagnosis, she insisted they have a different doctor (whom she called by name) examine me. The doctor did, and he said, "No, this is not a miscarriage. It's a polyp."

"What's that?" I asked hopefully.

"It's a non-cancerous tissue," he said. "We are going to remove it by tying a string around it and pulling it off. It's quite a simple procedure. You'll be fine."

I had the procedure an hour later, and like he said, I was completely fine.

I think about that moment a lot now, how my doctor cared enough to insist that I have a second opinion. I think about it and cannot help but associate it with race because Black women in the United States have the highest maternal mortality rate, 69.9 per 100,000 live births for 2021, almost three times the rate for White women, according to the Centers for Disease Control and Prevention. A rate I believe would drastically reduce if more White doctors paid attention, if they stopped and asked or even listened to the complaints of their Black patients.

Black women are so often dismissed, and that has cost so many of us our lives.

I stayed apprehensive for a few months, afraid one wrong move would affect my pregnancy. But as the months passed, our apprehension moved to acceptance and then excitement. We were having a second baby!

❋❋❋

Lil' James grew as excited for the baby as we did. He had been an only child for twelve years, so we thought having a baby brother would take some getting used to, but it didn't. Lil' James was expectant, completely overjoyed at the reality of being a big brother. I loved his energy, it was in direct contrast to mine at five years old when I found out Dorothy was having Rhoshay.

I had Jaylen five months before I finished my Masters. When he first came home, Lil' James was so excited, he kept trying to carry the baby. Afraid that he would hurt the baby, I refused him and forbade him from trying to carry his little brother when an adult wasn't there. His face had fallen when I said that, and after a few more tries, he stopped trying to touch or carry the baby. I think about that now, about how everyone else had been allowed to carry the baby but him. I wonder if that had made him feel as left out as I imagined and if that had been the catalyst that began everything.

One day, when Jaylen was eight months old, I needed to go to Home Depot. There was no one at home, and I didn't want to leave Lil' James home alone. So, I piled Jaylen and Lil' James into the car and drove to the store. When we got there, I contemplated taking them in but thought better of it. I wanted to be in and out as quickly as possible.

I turned to Lil' James, "Stay here, watch your little brother. I'll be out quickly."

I ran into the store and I cannot remember what I went into to pick up because what happened right after chased the memory from my head. I do remember that I kept thinking I had two children out in the car, and though I was mostly certain nothing would happen to them in the brief time I would be in the store, I didn't want to take any chances. Thankfully, the checkout counter was free, and I was out in five minutes. I started to walk to the car but froze in shock at what I saw. Lil' James had just slapped Jaylen hard in his face.

I hurried to the car as Jaylen's cries filled the air. Lil' James sat quietly in the back, staring at the baby like he hadn't hit him, like he didn't understand why he was suddenly crying. I picked Jaylen up and began to soothe him.

"You slapped him!" I asked Lil' James, more in shock than anger. "Why did you do that?"

He said nothing, just simply stared at us. His look was frightening, cold, and completely devoid of emotion. I drove home quickly, and that night, I reported Lil' James to his father. James's shock matched mine. He stormed over to Lil' James's room in anger. I hurried after him to control the situation. James was slow to anger; you had to poke him and come at him many times before he lost it. And he had lost it.

"You hit your baby brother!" he yelled at Lil' James. "You are grounded! Grounded!" He yelled at him some more and came back to the room fuming. "We've spoiled that kid," he said. "Hitting his baby brother? He didn't even look sorry."

I tried to talk to Lil' James after that to get to the root of his feelings, to try to understand what the baby could possibly have done to make him hit him. He wasn't a toddler. He wasn't a five-year-old unable to control his emotions, unable to tell the difference between right and wrong. He was 12 years old. He had to have known he could hurt the baby. Why had he done that?

But the more I tried to talk to Lil' James, the more he retreated from us. Soon, he began to keep the door to his room shut and only came out when he was hungry. I thought it had to be teenage angst; he was nearing thirteen years old, maybe that was it. I didn't know how boys behaved as teenagers. I grew up around little sisters, and Dorothy's strictness and mental instability kept us in check. I tried to imagine, to empathize with what Lil' James was feeling but often came up with a blank. So, I retreated and did my best to give him space. He was at that age I thought, that had to be it. What else could it be?

He continued like that, ignoring us and spending all his time in his room until one morning. He woke up groggy and irritated, and that led to a fight with his dad. Angry, he'd stormed out of the house to school and I remember shaking my head in rising anxiety as I prepared Jaylen for daycare. A few minutes later, I dropped Jaylen off at daycare and left for work. He was growing into a cute, chubby, happy baby, just like his brother had been.

I was just settling in for work when Lil' James's school called me.

"Yes," I answered.

A woman with a crisp voice said, "Mrs. Banks, we are calling to inquire why James isn't in school today."

My heart did a flip. "Excuse me. What do you mean he isn't in school?"

"We haven't seen him," she said.

"What do you mean you haven't seen him?! He left for school this morning!" I tried to remember what he was wearing when he left and my heart dived when I couldn't.

"Mrs. Banks, James hasn't been seen in school today," the woman repeated. "That's why we are calling. We thought you kept him back."

"I didn't," I said and hung up. My mind spun with a thousand possibilities as I called James at work. The distance from our house to Lil' James's school was barely ten minutes, so he didn't use the school bus. Ten minutes was such a brief time, but it was a long time too. All it took was less than one minute for some pervert to grab him, some pervert who probably had been watching him go back and forth to school. I thought about Chuck and how he had intentionally waited at that spot for me so he could taunt me and eventually show me his penis, and my heart raced. Dear God, I thought, dear Jesus.

James left work immediately after I called him. We called the police, and while they looked, we drove around the neighborhood looking. My mind raced some more as we searched. Maybe he ran away, I thought. But why would he run away?

"You shouldn't have yelled at him this morning!" I screamed at James after three hours of futile search. "He ran away because you yelled at him!"

James said nothing. I couldn't remember what they had argued about. I just remember both of them being so angry at each other.

"You shouldn't have yelled at him," I sobbed.

As night came, I thought of all the terrible things that could have happened to him. James insisted I go home and look after the baby while he kept on searching. Dorothy and my sisters had joined the search by now. I didn't want to go back home but Jaylen hadn't seen me all day. He was with a good babysitter, but by now, he was probably getting restless. I went home, released the babysitter, and sat by the phone with Jaylen in my arms, screening calls to make sure they didn't tie up the line in case James, the police, or Dorothy and my sisters called.

I called Momma crying, and she did her best to calm me. I hung up and called my father-in-law. "Pray for my son," I said. "He's missing,"

James called three hours later. It was 9 p.m., and I was on the verge of breaking down.

"Have you found him?" I asked

"No," James said, and I burst into tears.

"We will find him," James said, "don't worry. We will find him."

The doorbell rang an hour later, and I raced to the door to open it. Lil' James stood in the middle of two police officers with a defiant expression on his face. He stormed into the house before I could hug him or ask any questions, and I looked back at the police officers in gratitude, hurt, and confusion.

"Thank you so much," I said over and over.

"No worries, ma'am," they said. "You keep an eye on that one now. We found him at a drug house."

Chapter 15:
A Son's Turning Point

"They found him in a drug house," I told James when he returned home exhausted that night. "What was he doing in a drug house?" I asked James this question, as if he had the answer I'd be wracking my brain all night to find. What was Lil' James doing in a drug house?

James said nothing, but the intense worry in his eyes told me all I needed to know.

"Come rest," he said. " We will tackle this in the morning."

I followed him into the room, but I couldn't rest. I couldn't sleep. The police had found Lil' James in a drug house? A drug house? The thing (amongst many others) we had been trying to shield him from? That night, I tossed, turned, and thought.

About my father, how he'd worked for and with a drug crew and killed people for it.

About Dorothy and how she couldn't go a day without a pack of cigarettes. My memory opened, and I remembered a night I caught her doing cocaine. I remember her looking left and right before she bent down to snort, not seeing me as I hid behind the door and watched her, completely appalled.

I thought about Momma and her long addiction to alcohol.

Uncle Curtis and his addiction to heroin.

I thought about genetics and DNA and where I came from. Was it me? Had I somehow caused this? Had he picked this up from my bloodline? From my side of the family?

What was he doing in a drug house?

The next day, Dorothy called me. She was house hunting and needed my help. We had been house hunting for a month now. Every week, I would drive her around my neighborhood as she looked at houses and, just like that day in her bedroom, sigh longingly and say,

"I wish I could buy a house with a white picket fence."

I knew her desire to buy a house had been reignited after James and I purchased ours. And it made me happy that instead of wishing for things, she had taken a step to make it happen for herself.

As we drove around that day, I told her we found Lil' James in a drug house. She and my sisters had gone home tired after being informed we'd found Lil' James. I'd been too shocked then to tell them where.

"Drug house?" she asked in surprise. "How he find a drug house in this uppity neighborhood?"

I sighed. Our neighborhood was hardly uppity. It was a barely thirty-minute car ride to Carr Square. Also, it was easy to find something if you really, genuinely wanted it, and that was what worried me. Why did Lil' James feel the need to look for a drug house? How long had he been going there?

He still hadn't spoken to us since the police brought him back home. He was angry at us, and that made me angry. He was the one who had run away to a drug house, and he was angry at us?

Dorothy and I drove some more and we stopped just opposite a cute little house with a white picket fence. It had a for sale sign in front of it, and Dorothy sighed longingly at it.

"I bet it has a nice basement," she said.

Basement. I thought about the month before Jaylen was born. James and I had unanimously decided to convert Lil' James's bedroom into a nursery for the baby and convert the basement into a bedroom for Lil' James. We had gone back and forth about it, wondering how and when to tell Lil' James. What if he felt excluded? Rejected? Ignored? What if he threw a tantrum and refused to leave his room? Jaylen had been unplanned, a happy surprise and getting a new house with more rooms hadn't been in the budget. But when we finally told Lil' James, gently and even apologetically, he shrugged and said, "So I get the whole basement to myself? Just me?"

"Just you," his father agreed with a huge smile of relief. He proceeded to remodel the entire basement, turning it into a teen paradise. Lil' James loved it when he saw it. But had he? Had he been hiding how he truly felt, or had we just seen what we'd chosen to see?

"You think I can afford this?" Dorothy asked.

I gave the house one more look and sighed tiredly. "I don't think so, Dorothy."

She sighed right back. "That's what I thought."

"What should I do about Lil' James?" I asked.

She shrugged. "Keep an eye on him. Check his friends, too. Check them."

Back home that day, James and I talked at the dinner table while Lil' James sulked in his room. We traced back his steps, broke down his routine, and tried to figure out who he'd been spending time together with. I thought about his friends from school; they seemed normal enough. Awkward pre-teens and teenagers, or was there someone else? Someone we didn't know? Someone who had introduced him to drugs? There had to be, I thought. He was twelve years old. What did he even know about buying and using drugs? It had to be a friend, some friend. I was certain of it.

The more we looked, the more we found he had a separate set of friends outside of school. The kind of friends that reminded me of Eric and how he'd stolen Dorothy's gun and naked pictures. I still cringed a little every time I remembered that episode. Lil' James had been spending his after-school time with these types of friends and we had somehow missed it.

After finding this out, James suggested we take him out of the public school and put him into a private one. I agreed.

"This way," he said, "he won't spend time together with his old friends anymore. They can't influence him if he's not there to be influenced. They can't."

***

We followed Lil' James's change of school with the start of therapy. My family thought it was strange and unnecessary. Dorothy had simply snorted when I told her. She had taken a loan from the bank and bought herself a cute little house ten minutes away from mine, and now she was mostly focused on tending to it. But Momma had tried harder to discourage me. She simply wanted me to pray harder for him because therapy was White people's thing.

"You don't want to be telling no stranger your business," she said.

She leaned more toward God and prayer now, especially with Bill gone. Prayer and more prayer were her solution to everything. While I believed in prayer and God, I knew enough to know you had to show up and put in your part of the work.

So, I ignored all of them and put Lil' James into therapy. How many times as a child had I wished I could simply talk to someone?

Someone who got it? Who understood? Who could help me figure things out or, at the very least, just listen? I wanted to understand Lil' James, to be the one he ran to when he was hurt, angry, or sad. I wanted to be the one he confessed to why he needed the drugs. Maybe it was recreational, maybe it was deeper; I desperately wanted to know. But he shut me out, growing even more angry and sullen by the day. So maybe, maybe a stranger could succeed where I'd failed.

I'd look at him, sitting by himself or pretending to read a book so he wouldn't talk to us and try to figure out what to say to him, how to say it to him. My heart would ache so badly for him, for the little boy who had looked at me with a twinkle in his eyes. Who had hopped happily beside me while holding my hand. Who had called his grandmother 'honey' because his grandfather did. I remembered how he wouldn't let James leave for work until James gave him his forehead kisses and, of course, how James was always so happy to do it.

Somewhere, and we didn't know where, in between buying a new house, getting my masters, getting a new job, and having a surprise baby, we'd lost that little boy. And now, I was desperate to find him. Maybe therapy would help me do that. Maybe therapy would bring him back to us.

I told Lil' James about therapy, and he seemed okay with it. An hour a week? No problem. I'd expected him to fight me on it, to slam the door to his room and not speak to us for days or weeks. But he agreed wholeheartedly.

James went to drop him off that first day and shook the hand of the white therapist who promised him she would get to the root of the situation.

"These things happen," she said. "Give it time, just give it some time."

James nodded and went out to wait in the car.

That first day, even though I knew it would take more than an afternoon to fix Lil' James, I sat on pins and needles, waiting for the therapist to call me. Waiting for her to get back to me and tell me she'd fixed my child, and all was well now. But Lil' James came back home that day, the same as he left and the same every day after that. His mood improved, but not his behavior. He got ruder and even more snappy; his attitude started making me anxious.

After four sessions, I reached out to the therapist and asked her how the sessions were going.

"You need to give him more space," she said.

"What?" I asked in confusion.

"He's a growing teenager, and he needs his space. He feels suffocated. You need to give him more freedom, Mom."

She said the word 'mom' in a derisive tone and I was too stunned to speak. She honestly couldn't mean that. I knew what it meant to not have freedom, to be suffocated, and not have any friends. I knew because Dorothy made sure of that. She controlled my friends and hours. She decided who she wanted me to be friends with and where she wanted me to go. I'd hated that, hated that I couldn't go out with my friends, couldn't walk the park without worrying that Dorothy would find me and slap my ass back home. I'd hated it enough to swear never to do it to my child, and now here, this therapist was suggesting that I was suffocating him. With what? He had the whole basement to himself!

"What about the baby?" I said. "He hit him one time. That can't be because I'm suffocating him."

"He loves his brother. It's a sibling thing; that's completely normal. If you give him more space, give him some more breathing room, it will improve things. Stop suffocating him, Mom, give him space to breathe."

There was that derisive tone again.

"Okay," I said, trying to control my breathing. "Okay."

"Also," she continued in an even more condescending tone. "I'm going to recommend you see a therapist so they can teach you how to parent a teenager. Parenting a teenager can be hard. It gets tougher as they get older."

I was upset by her assessment of the situation. But then I thought, what if she is right? What if I don't know how to parent a teenager? So, I spoke to the therapist she recommended. We talked on the phone once and she basically said the same thing. "Give him more space. Extend his curfew. Let him show you he can be responsible."

James and I did that and held our breaths to see if anything would change. But it didn't. Lil' James was good the first couple of weeks, but after that, the calls started coming in: he was being disrespectful in class, he wasn't doing his homework, he was fighting the other kids, he was showing up late to class. For every call we got, James would try to talk to him. When gentle talking didn't work, he took to yelling at him.

We gave him space like the therapist wanted, but he took to staying out and coming home late. When he got to eighth grade; he started skipping school altogether. I tried everything I could to pull him back, but it was as if the more I did, the more he slipped away from me.

We took him back to public school after that because maybe he missed his friends and if he were around them again, he would act better. But he didn't. He missed classes even more and found even more drug houses. I could feel him slipping and slipping and slipping away. Until, in order to catch him, I told James we had to move.

"Let's get a house in the suburbs," I said. "There are no drug houses there. We can save him if we just move."

"Buying a new house right now is a lot," James said. "We may not be able to afford it."

"We will find a way," I said desperately. I was going back to school, trying to get a second master's in health care administration. I knew that would make a difference in my income. I was hopeful, no, certain of it.

" Let's move," I begged James. "This may be the only way to save our child. Let's move."

So, we did, abandoning everything we'd ever known, carrying with us a hope that this was it, this was the thing that would reset Lil' James.

Chapter 16:
BREAKING THE CYCLE

We moved fifty miles away to St. Charles County, in a suburb called Lake St. Louis. I wanted to be as far away from Carr Square as possible, from the people and things making Lil' James into what he was becoming. He had sulked as we packed, unhappy that he was losing his friends, and that made me secretly happy because he was losing the friends that were making him reject his family.

The day before we moved, I took a walk around our old house. All our boxes were packed and stacked and the rooms were empty. It still amazed me that we went from our tiny apartment to this house. I got to the living room, sighed, and sat in the middle of the floor.

This house had sparked new beginnings for us. It also revealed things about us we otherwise wouldn't have known. It was in this house I discovered that James was a genius at remodeling. He had taken the dingy basement and turned it into a gorgeous, homey teenage room for Lil' James and a family hang-out room with a built-in large-screen TV for us. I remember walking into it after he was done and marveling that my husband could do something like this. He had stood there shyly, trying to downplay his work, but I knew that instead of his miserable job as facility service supervisor (he got promoted over the years), this was it. This was the thing he was supposed to be doing.

"You need to quit your job," I said. "You need to quit and go into remodeling houses full time."

He shook his head before I finished talking. "Jaylen and Lil' James are still too young to have both parents out of the house all the time. They need to be able to come home to one of us every day."

"Also," he'd added with finality. "Starting a business will take a lot of money. We can't spare that right now."

He was right, but I wasn't about to let him let go of something that made his eyes shine with excitement. I owed James. He'd picked up the slack when I went to college, working at night so he could stay with Lil' James when I was in class. He did the same when I went for both of my master's degrees and every time afterward when I needed to travel for work. He never complained, never made me feel guilty, and was always there when I needed him.

"Okay, promise me," I said, "that when I start to make as much as both of us are earning now, you will quit your job and go into remodeling."

"Rhoda..."

"Promise."

"Fine," he said. "I promise." I could tell he was secretly excited. Even now, he was anticipating putting in some work at our new home. He'd tried to hide his excitement, but I could see it clear as the shiny oak pool table he'd installed in the basement of this house.

This house was also the catalyst that had led Dorothy to purchase her own house ten minutes away from mine. I still remember the look on her face when she stepped into her home for the first time—she was coming home, literally. She was getting the thing she'd always wanted, the thing she never thought she'd have. I wanted to frame the awe and satisfaction on her face and hang it on my bedroom wall. The house hadn't been much, just a cute two-bedroom that didn't come with a fridge and a basement that flooded when it rained. But Dorothy loved it. She painstakingly chose every piece of furniture and to show my excitement for her, I'd bought her a fridge.

It was here that I found out Dorothy had a green thumb and a knack for raising healthy beautiful plants. She was happy here, content in a way I'd never seen, and I'd surprised myself by spending almost every weekend with her at her home. I came one time and found her playing Anita Baker at a near-splitting volume. She used to do that a lot when we were kids. She would play Maze and Frankie Beverly, Gladys Knight, and The Pips when she needed to cook or do chores. But somehow, here, the music felt different.

"It's not for me," she said, laughing happily when I asked about the volume. "It's for my plants. They love music. It makes them grow."

I laughed, but she shook her head sternly, "It's true. Have you seen any plants healthier than mine?" I studied her plants in amusement. She was right, they were healthy.

Being in her own home made her happy, fun, and jovial. She was a different person, and it made me sad I never got this woman while growing up.

With her new home ready, I thought she would be happy to host Thanksgiving that year, but she refused. It didn't make any sense to me. Why take such painstaking care of your home if you won't let your family enjoy it with you? When I refused to have Thanksgiving at my house, she got upset. I was tired of doing all the work while everyone came, ate, and left. I wanted to be a guest. To punish me, Dorothy agreed to have Thanksgiving at her house but didn't invite me. It completely stung me. She'd invited everyone in the family except for me. I thought our relationship had grown, changed, and matured.

When Rhoshay urged her to invite me because "it was just wrong I'd be excluded," I turned down the invitation. It hurt even more that she'd waited to be urged to invite me.

I thought of Jaylen and his tiny little feet as he'd walked for the first time in this living room. We had jumped in excitement, and he had laughed victoriously. Jaylen was different, not the bad little boy I'd hoped for in Lil' James. He was sensitive and gentle, and I found myself being increasingly thankful for that.

I realized then how deeply I was going to miss this house. And I worried, too. What if moving didn't make a difference with Lil' James? What if this change made everything so much worse?

✳✳✳

Our new home was beautiful. It was a 3,000 square feet two-story home with four bedrooms, three bathrooms, a family room, a dining room, a bonus room, and an unfinished basement that James remodeled into the most stunning second family room. Our home was in a beautiful suburb with manicured lawns, big department stores, strip malls, shopping malls, and suburban office parks. I immediately felt guilty for living here, as if I were doing something I wasn't supposed to. I'd felt this way in our last home, too—an irrational feeling of guilt that I was doing better than most of my family and many of my Black peers. This feeling insisted I was never supposed to make it out. I'd felt like that when I started to make more money, except here, it felt worse because I was doing it among White people, who were the majority of my neighbors. I found out later that what I was feeling was survivor's guilt.

Our family was one of two Black families on our street, but our neighbors were very friendly. One of them, our neighbor from across the street, the Abernathy's, used to live in our old neighborhood and had moved here a couple of years before us. They had twins, and Jaylen immediately became friends with them, while James and I became friends with their parents. It felt good, like we had brought some part of St. Louis with us.

We were just settling in when Momma made a big move, too.

After Bill died, she moved my uncle Freddie into a nursing home. He had lived with her all his life, his epilepsy tethering them to each other. Freddie had seemed unable to exist outside of Momma and I often wondered if Momma ever encouraged him to. After Freddie moved to the nursing home, we found an apartment complex for seniors for Momma. It was colorful and fun, designed with features to entertain and engage the seniors. The complex made me think of daycare and made me realize how our beginning is so similar to our end. Except that often, we are nurtured and unconditionally loved at the beginning but discarded and forgotten toward the end. I never wanted Momma to feel like that.

A month after Momma moved into the complex, she started acting strangely. She would go to the grocery store and call me, saying all the meat was black. She would call me in the middle of the day to tell me that all the people who lived in her building had red eyes, and they wouldn't stop looking at her. She had gone back to seeing the hanks, too. They were everywhere she turned.

We immediately admitted her into a mental hospital. After a month, the doctor told us her hallucinations were a result of her undiagnosed depression, which had led her to become paranoid.

"This happens all the time," the doctor said. "Especially when a person experiences a big change and has spent all their lives taking care of other people."

Caring for Bill and Freddie had kept her demons at bay, and without them, they kept swarming around her. The doctors put her on medication, and she got better after a month, but the doctors advised that she shouldn't be left by herself.

She needed to live with one of us. But I knew with Lil' James acting up, I couldn't realistically add Momma to the mix. I went over options in my mind, but my younger sister, Rayneika, stepped in and happily took Momma to live with her.

❋❋❋

Despite the friendliness of our new neighborhood, it took us a while to get settled in St. Charles. When we finally did, Lil' James's attitude started up again.

He was the only one in the family who didn't take to St. Charles. He approached it with a mixture of indifference and disdain, not caring for one minute and completely despising it the next. His attitude upsets me. I knew he was missing his friends, and I knew St. Charles didn't have the character and sense of community that St. Louis did, but it was peaceful, receptive, very friendly and, importantly, less likely to have a drug house. I thought of ways to get Lil' James settled in St. Charles and grew frustrated when I came up with a blank. His attitude got worse, and I grew even more frustrated. When I pointed it out to Momma, she advised me to give him more time.

"He's going to come around, Rhoda," she said. "You just give him more time and pray for him."

So, I did. I prayed for him and gave him time like Momma advised, gave him space like the therapist advised but, he kept getting worse.

I thought it'd be impossible to find a drug house here. This was the suburbs and, even if not impossible, immensely difficult. But somehow, Lil' James found them, along with his people: young, defiant teenagers experimenting with everything that came their way. I started to find weed in his pockets when I did laundry and, in his room, when I went to drop his clothes. My panic grew, and I fought the urge to search his room. I was advised to give him space, to give him time and I knew searching his room would alienate him. But James and I were at our wits end; nothing was working. We grounded him more, but he snuck out. We took away his allowance, and he still found a way to buy weed. It didn't matter what we did, he seemed intent on doing whatever he wanted, which was predominantly skipping school or finding the wrong crowd. Everything we did to stop him made him worse, and sometimes, I imagined him laughing in the face of our efforts to rein him in.

It got worse when he turned sixteen. Before long, he stayed out two to three days at a time. So much so that James and I would drive around the neighborhood looking for him. Our new neighbors looked at us with pity, and it infuriated me. We were one of two Black families living in this neighborhood. Lil' James's behavior was helping feed into whatever stereotype our neighborhood may have had about Black people. I imagined them judging us in their perfect white homes and got infuriated all over again.

One day, Lil' James stayed out for days and after a particularly long and tiring search, we found him spending time together with a group of friends and brought him home. The moment we stepped into the house, James began to yell at him. Screaming, cursing, and threatening, and in tears, I told him to stop. The cursing and the screaming had reminded me of Dorothy, of how she'd cuss and scream at us for no reason. Or how she'd put us out when she eventually got tired of screaming and cursing. It was scaring Jaylen, too. He didn't understand why we wouldn't stop screaming. James had been furious with me for trying to stop him, which had led to another round of screaming.

"You can't do that!" he screamed in frustration; his face clouded with exhaustion. "We have been up all night searching for him. You can't undermine me in front of him like that! We need to be united. We've been calm. We've given him all the space. If we don't get angry, he's not going to stop!"

"You don't have to yell at him like that!" I snapped.

"That's exactly what he needs! He's skipping school and staying out for days. Days! Did you see the kids we found him with? Did you see them?!"

Of course I saw them. They had been rough-looking and drug-addled. Not the kind of kids I thought I'd find in the suburbs. I'd been too stunned to speak when I saw him with them. Yet, he seemed so relaxed, like he was exactly where he was supposed to be.

That night, after James went to sleep, I walked anxiously to Lil' James's room. His door was slightly ajar, and he was awake and on his phone. I felt relieved when I saw that. Some part of me had feared he had snuck out again. I was about to go back to my room when I stopped. Taking a deep breath, I knocked softly and opened the door before he told me to come in. I didn't want to give him a chance to tell me to stay out. He turned his face when he saw me, and my chest squeezed with hurt.

"You need to stop," I said firmly.

He said nothing.

"It's disrespectful when you stay out late like that, and we worry when you don't call. When you stay gone for days and don't even think to call. You need to stop."

"I'm not doing anything, Mom," he said.

"What do you need the drugs for," I asked. "Why do you need them?"

"It's just weed, Mom. It's from the earth. It's pure." He said it with so much confidence, like he'd spent time researching the origin and benefits of weed.

I controlled my temper. "It's not just weed. It's not pure. They add things to it that can really mess you up. Is that what you want?"

"You don't get it," he said as if I was too old to understand anything.

I wanted to tell him to make me get it, make me understand why he needed to use the drug. But I knew he was done talking to me. So, instead, I said, "Your behavior is becoming unacceptable. You need to stop."

Insignificant things began to go missing after that, a pair of my shoes, an expensive perfume James had given me, and bottles of whiskey from the kitchen cabinet. Lil' James was taking them and selling them to buy drugs. I thought the only thing he smoked by then was weed, but I would find out later it was much more.

When these things went missing, we had no doubt Lil' James had taken them because he didn't try to hide it. James would get angry and yell at Lil' James, and I would tell him to stop. It always turned into a screaming match, him screaming at Lil' James, me screaming at him to stop and Jaylen crying in the corner. It was a horrible, desperate situation that always ended with everyone being furious at each other, except for Jaylen. He just wanted all of us to be happy.

A few days after the last screaming match, I woke up at 2 a.m., made my way to the kitchen to get some water, looked out the driveway, and found my car was missing. I dropped my cup in shock and raced back into the room to tell James. It was a new car.

I shook James awake. "My car's gone," I said.

"What?" he asked sleepily.

"My car is gone."

The sleep left his eyes as realization dawned. "Lil' James took it," he said.

"No, I don't think…"

"Lil' James took it!"

"He doesn't even have his driver's license yet." Fear rippled down my spine. What if he gets pulled over by the police? A young Black boy driving an expensive new car, he was a magnet for racist police officers. What if he gets into an accident? What if he killed someone?

James was already putting on his clothes, "I told you, "He said. "I told you we needed to be harder on him."

Some of my worries dissolved into anger when he said that. I had defended Lil' James every time his father came at him, defended him so much that he now had no respect for his father. James was right; we should be harder on him. I dialed his number, and he picked up on the second ring. I was surging with anger by this time.

"Do you have my car?" I asked.

"Yeah," he said casually.

"Bring it back this instant!"

He came back several minutes later, and when he did, I had the police officers waiting for him. I was ready to press charges. Maybe that would teach him some sense, make him stop, pull him back. But the police convinced me not to.

"You don't want him in the system," the police officer said, and his colleague nodded in agreement. "It will follow him for the rest of his life."

They turned to Lil' James who was standing at a corner, looking at us like he couldn't possibly be bothered.

"It's obvious your parents have provided you with a good life. Do the right thing," he said. "Stop before you ruin it."

But a few days later, having a sense that he was up to something, I came home and found Lil' James home from school with five other teenagers, four boys and one girl. They were smoking weed and eating frozen pizza. The music was turned on so loud they hadn't heard me come in. The moment they did, they tried to sneak out. I ordered them all to leave, and Lil' James left with them.

He was gone for five days. He didn't call or text, and I almost lost my mind with worry. When he swaggered into the house on the sixth day, completely unbothered, I felt rage bubble up in me again. He made his way to his room, and I cut him short furiously. Standing before him, breathing angrily, I looked into his eyes, and they reminded me so much of Dorothy—the way they glazed over when she was angry and daring you to say something dumb to her. I felt something in me snap.

"Get out!" I screamed.

He looked at me in disbelief, and I doubled down.

"If you are going to live here, you need to respect us and our rules. Stop bringing strangers into our house! And for God's sake, stop stealing our stuff! If you cannot do that, then get your stuff and leave!"

I watched his eyes as they hardened, and I felt panic climb quickly through my spine. I wanted to take back my words. Tell him I didn't mean that, tell him of course he could stay. But I couldn't because he looked at me at that moment like he despised me beyond words.

He walked quietly into his room, packed a bag, and walked out without sparing me a glance.

The slamming of the door rocked me to my core, and I broke down in tears.

Chapter 17:
Crossroads of Parenthood

The night after Lil' James left, I tossed and turned in bed. It felt like there was a heavy, indescribable weight pressing down on my chest, but no matter how tossed and turned, it wouldn't ease up. At three in the morning, I gave up sleeping, walked into the kitchen for a cup of water, opened the fridge, found leftover pizza sitting on the top shelf, and burst into tears. I heaved until I thought my chest would crumble from the weight.

The day Dorothy kicked me out, I'd walked out in righteous anger, furious at her and desperate to prove to her I could do life without her, and I did. But as I stared at that leftover pizza, I understood it. She cried the day I left because I broke her heart. Her tears weren't for the right reasons, but a broken heart doesn't know that. It can't always tell the difference.

Only your child can break your heart like that. Whether you are a good mom or a bad mom, having your child walk away from you will always be heartbreaking.

Unable to go back to sleep, I sat in the living room and dialed Lil' James's phone. It rang but he didn't pick up, and after the sixth ring, I gave up and made my way to Jaylen's room. He was fast asleep in a fetal position. He slept so differently from Lil' James, so carefully curled up as if he were afraid spreading out would expose him to some type of danger. Lil' James, on the other hand, slept with careless abandon, except for the nights I'd come into his room and find him curled up as if he'd had a bad dream and was trying to protect himself from it. Gently, I pulled the blanket more securely over Jaylen.

'Raising a baby isn't going to be easy,' Momma said. What had made me think I could succeed at the thing the women before me had failed at?

***

Lil' James moved into a trailer park with the White family, and the only reason I knew was because he came back a few weeks later, strung out and broke up to tell us. Even completely strung out, he still defended the thing ruining his life.

"Marijuana isn't bad, ma," he said. "It's from the earth. It's nature's herb."

I tried to hold back tears when I saw him, but not Jaylen. He cried when he saw his older brother. He was five years old at the time, at an age when most little kids worshiped their older siblings. But he'd looked at Lil' James with such fear and sadness that I'd eventually broken down in tears, too.

Lil' James came back a lot more after that, and every time he did, he stole something. He'd take food or cash he saw around the house, and if we tried to ask him when he was coming home, he would get angry. He'd be smiling one minute, and the next, he was furious and knocking over a flower vase. Even his smiles weren't happy. They seemed manic as if he were smiling because the alternative to that was worse. I wondered then if this was more than a teenage rebellion. If he was… mentally unwell. Was it the drugs affecting his mood, or were they masking something deeper? But the words were hard for me to think, hard for me to accept, so

I didn't. Teenagers acted like this sometimes; they were rebellious and irrational. Some even emancipated from their parents. Lil' James was just going through a phase, a phase that was actively ruining his life. But he would come back eventually. He had to.

But the signs were all there: the firecracker he'd set off in the living room when he was seven, slapping his baby brother when he was twelve, occasionally sinking into depressive silence when he was thirteen, experimenting with drugs, and turning up the music in his room so loud; even at night as if he was trying to drown out his thoughts. The signs were all there, but I didn't want to see them. No mother wants to admit that their child is mentally unwell.

The more Lil' James came to the house, the more I begged him to stay. He would for a day or two before he stormed out in rage over a fight. I never knew what to say when I was around him; I never knew how to say it so I wouldn't set him off. Eventually, his anger and outbursts got so much that James banned him from coming over.

"You have a little brother," he screamed in anger. "You think it's okay for him to see you like this! Until you are ready to be a part of this family, stay out!"

After that, Lil' James didn't show up at our house for weeks and when he did, he made sure to show up when I'd be the one home.

My neighbors looked at me with sympathy, and my friends kept telling me to go get him. As if I could just show up at the trailer park, put him into the car and drive him home. As if he wasn't turning into a grown man who was rapidly terrifying me. Eventually, my friends stopped saying anything because every time they did, I'd burst into tears.

His final year rolled around and with that, a new worry. Before the attitude and the drugs, Lil' James was a straight-A student. His report cards always made me happy, and his teachers were full of praise for him. Now, they expressed deep disappointment as they watched his potential go to waste. Lil' James had missed classes so much that the possibility of graduating was slim.

I called the principal to see how the situation could be salvaged.

"He can still graduate," he said.

"He can?"

"Yes. He's a smart kid, and despite everything happening, his grades are above average. He'll graduate if he takes his final exams."

I made it my mission to get Lil' James to take his finals. I called, begged, and even threatened.

"Just take your finals," I said. "Go take it, and I won't ask you to do anything else." I knew if he skipped this part, if he didn't take it now, it would be so much harder to come back. He finally relented, went, took the exams, and passed every single one. He called to tell me he'd done it, and on the day of his graduation, I sat in the front row cheering with the other parents as he went to receive his diploma. Afterward, he brought his diploma to me, wearing the new suit James had bought him.

"Here," he said and handed it to me. "You the one who wanted me to graduate."

"Thank you," I said and hugged him.

We went to eat afterward at Uncle Bill's Pancake House, a staple in Lake St. Louis. There was a small crowd; our family, James's sister, and her kids, and some of Lil' James's friends from school came with us. We found a nice spot and proceeded to eat heartily as we laughed and joked. Lil' James looked so happy and content. He looked like the son I remember. I remember thinking how normal everything seemed that day, how I felt so strongly that we'd got Lil'

James back. James handed him three hundred dollars cash we'd kept for his graduation, and he received it with a grateful smile on his face. My heart had never felt warmer.

After he left with his friends, I took his diploma back home, hung it in the family room, and stared at it. When I look at it now, I don't see a degree of completion. I see us at the Pancake House, laughing and eating together. I had my son back that day. I hold on tightly to that now because I lost him afterward.

✢✢✢

After his graduation, we barely saw him for months after that. We knew we could potentially run into him at a supermarket or grocery store, but we rarely ever did, especially after he moved from the trailer park into an apartment complex not far from us. It was ironic that he lived so close to us and yet was intentional about staying away from us like he'd rejected us and never wanted to see us again. It was a terrible feeling to know that I could run into my child, and he'd walk past me like a stranger. He already looked like one. Every time he appeared at the house, he appeared thinner, his eyes looked smaller, like slits, and he stopped shaving. I'd look at him and try to recall his sweet face when he was a baby. The way he'd laugh innocently and look at me in awe or hold my palm tightly whenever we walked down the street. It was hard to believe that version of my son was lost forever; even harder and scarier to think this version of him was all there ever would be.

After Lil' James moved out of the house, everyone blamed us. We had spoiled him, they said. We hadn't spoiled him enough. We had given him too much freedom, or we didn't give him enough. We weren't strict enough; we were too strict.

But no one judged me harder than me. Many nights, I thought, if I had just let James discipline him, if I hadn't stopped him, if we hadn't moved here, if I hadn't given him that ultimatum, if I had begged harder; maybe he would have stayed.

Soon, it became impossible for me to have a conversation with a friend about Lil' James without hearing the words:

"Go get your son back, Rhoda."

"You are not trying hard enough, Rhoda."

"Don't you want him back, Rhoda?"

Their statements felt like conviction, a judgment. You've failed as a mother, Rhoda. You've failed, you've failed, you've failed.

Eventually, crying one day, I called Dorothy. "Help me," I said. "Help me get my son back."

I'm not sure why I called her. In retrospect as I think about it, I realized I could have called someone else. But she's my mother, and at that moment, I felt this pull toward her, the indescribable need to be comforted the way only a mother could comfort her child. I wanted her to tell me her heart had broken when I moved out, too, but I had turned out all right, and Lil' James would, too.

She didn't say any of that. Instead, she came over, got into the car and together we went to look for Lil' James. We stopped at the apartment complex first, but he wasn't there.

Embarrassed by my phone call, we didn't say anything to each other in the car. We drove, looking out our individual sides of the window to find Lil' James. We found him quicker than I expected, and I almost cried in relief. He looked scruffy, but he was alive and well.

"Let me talk to him," Dorothy said. "He doesn't look like he want to talk to you."

It stung when she said it, but she was right. Lil' James didn't want to talk to me. He turned his face away when he saw me, and that broke my heart even more.

Dorothy walked toward him to talk to him, and standing so close together, I saw the resemblance again. The matching stubborn stance, the set jaw, the eyes that look so angry, so rebellious. I knew it made no sense, but somehow, while I slept, it was as if Dorothy had taken my baby and replaced him with herself.

They talked for some minutes, with Lil' James shaking his head and pulling away for most of it. I tried to go to him, but he gave me a look that froze me in my steps. He didn't need me, and he wasn't coming home.

On the way home, Dorothy kept a firm grasp on the wheel and her eyes on the road and next to her, with my head against the windshield, I cried.

Chapter 18:
It's in the DNA

After that, I threw myself into the things I could control: work, paying off our mortgage, and school. I was pursuing a Master's in Healthcare Administration. I'd already gotten a Master's in Human Resources Training and Development but had been unlucky in securing a job in it. So, I decided to move up in healthcare since I was already in it. I'd been working in it even as a cashier at the Barnes Jewish Hospital Garage. I hoped if I got a Master's in Health Care Administration, I could go into administration in one of the hospitals. So, I worked hard to get my degree. This required more hours at work and studying. James was still the primary parent because I traveled so much, but I made up for that by spending all of my available time with Jaylen.

Increasingly, I saw that James was getting miserable at his job. He complained to me about it constantly. He'd worked his way up from janitor to team lead to supervisor and then Director of Facilities. But his promotion only came with more stress. He dealt with a lot of employee issues. He oversaw the housekeeping staff and had to deal with the fallout whenever they stole, showed up late for work, fought, or slept on the job.

James had to deal with a ton of complaints, and every time he had to write an employee up or fire them, he had to deal with their union representative.

The more miserable he got, the harder I worked so he could quit. I poured all of myself into that goal because his problem was something I could handle, something I could fix by putting in more hours at work with the goal of a new promotion. It felt good to work on something I could fix.

The harder I worked, the more I suggested he quit his job. But every time I did, he'd shake his head before I finished talking.

"The mortgage on this house is twice what we used to pay on the last one." he'd say. "I'm not going to let you do that yourself. Plus, you travel so much. Who's going to look after Jaylen when you are not here?"

Sometimes, I wondered if he was fearful of the expenses or of failing if he went out on his own. So, I stopped talking about it and just focused on working on it. He wouldn't have an excuse when I finally had enough for him to quit.

The harder I worked, the less I thought about Lil' James. But he remained in the corners of my mind, springing up when I ran into an old classmate of his or when Jaylen did something at his age that reminded me of a young Lil' James. That's how it went until Lil' James came back into our lives again, in the most shocking way possible.

I was at a work conference. I had just signed into my hotel room when I got a text from Lil' James. My chest tightened in panic as I opened it. It'd been so long since I got a text from him. Opening the text, I scanned it in confusion. It was broken and incoherent, a string of lines, none of them making sense. Petrified, I texted back immediately.

"Are you alright?"

I waited anxiously for a reply, and when, after five minutes, I didn't get any, I set my phone aside and began to prepare for the conference.

I was already in the middle of it when Lil' James called me. Stunned, I answered immediately.

"Hello," I said. But there was no response. All I got was heavy breathing at the end of the line. Panicked, I called his name, "James. James. James!"

The last "James" drew stares my way; I excused myself and went out to the lobby of the hotel. Thankfully, there were few people there, each focused on the business that brought them. I redialed Lil' James's number and waited for him to pick up but he didn't. After trying a third time, I started to dial my husband's number when a text from Lil' James came in, and then another, and then another. Before I knew it, there were several lines of incoherent text. Bewildered, I went back into the conference and showed the texts to a nurse friend of mine. She scanned the texts quickly and said,

"Rhoda, you need to get your son to a mental hospital. This is a psychotic break."

The words echoed in my head. "What?" I mumbled.

"I've seen things like this before. You need to take him to a mental hospital before he hurts himself or someone else."

Mental hospital? Mental hospital?? My son wasn't crazy.

"Rhoda!" She said sharply, snapping me out of it.

Excusing myself, I went back out to call my husband. He picked up on the first ring.

"Hey," he said.

"You need to go get Lil' James," I said. "He's having a psychotic break."

"Excuse me?"

"He's been sending me incoherent texts all day, and I just showed it to my friend, and she suggested that Lil' James may be having a psychotic break. You need to go get him."

James hung up before I said anything else. Unable to focus at the conference, I went back to the hotel room and googled 'psychotic break.' I scrolled up and down the search results, trying to get as much information as I could before panic overwhelmed me. Not getting what I wanted, I changed my questions.

'Can a psychotic break be treated? Is it hereditary? Can it be cured?'

I thought about his behavior in the last few years and typed, 'What are the symptoms?' As the results loaded, I couldn't help but wonder, had they been there all along? Had the symptoms been there, and we'd mistaken them all for teenage rebellion? Exhausted, I set my phone aside and paced. Hoping Lil' James had called or sent another text, I picked my phone back up to check, but he hadn't. Even more exhausted, I fell asleep and woke up an hour later, but there were still no messages from him. My heart sank even more. What if something had happened to him? What if he was dead? Was that why James hadn't called me? He didn't know how to tell me something bad had happened.

I called him. "How is he?"

"I was about to call you," James said. "He doesn't look good,"

My heart dropped. "What do you mean?"

"I think you need to come back home," he said. "He doesn't look good."

❋❋❋

When James and I were dating, he told me about his older brother, Elijah. Elijah was normal until he turned eighteen, went to a party, and someone spiked his drink with a drug. He drank it, had a psychotic break, and from there, it was chaos. He got violent at the slightest things and attacked anyone who tried to calm him down. He was taken to a mental hospital and diagnosed as bipolar. Medicated, he was able to live a normal life. Unmedicated, he was violent and dangerous to himself and the people around him. He stayed heavily medicated for most of his life, with episodes here and there, but was able to hold down an apartment and a job until he died in his mid-sixties from lung cancer.

I found the story fascinating when James told me because I'd met Elijah, and aside from being a terrible loner, he was as normal as he could be. He was truly kind and quiet. Also, I really found the story fascinating because some of the behaviors he described of Elijah were traits Dorothy displayed sometimes. Did that mean she was bipolar, too? I never witnessed Elijah's episodes. They were just scary and sometimes funny stories I'd heard. So, it never occurred to me that mental illness could be hereditary or that my son would one day become a victim.

With Elijah, the stories were fascinating, but with my son, it was devastating.

James found Lil' James high out of his mind and completely disassociated from reality. He immediately checked him into a mental facility about three miles from the house, and we weren't allowed to see him for the first week.

Walking into that mental hospital to see him that second week felt like walking on hot and cold coals simultaneously. It was painful as if every nerve in my body was being attacked.

How could this have happened? Why was this happening?

And yet, on the other hand, it made sense and brought a twisted kind of relief. He hadn't been the way he was because he hated us and our family. He was that way because he couldn't help it.

Still, it felt like such a random, mean thing to happen to me, to him, to all of us. I thought about twenty-year-old me and how excited she'd been to have a child, to create the family she'd never had, and I laughed, loud and long enough for James to look suspiciously at me. We thought we knew everything, dear God! We were so stupid.

We entered the treatment room to find Lil' James sitting at a table. He looked clean, calm, and heavily medicated. He looked good, better than I had seen him in a while, but still, I stared at him like I couldn't recognize him. When did he become this person? What happened to my son?

"Mr. and Mrs. Banks, please have a seat," the doctor said.

We took the ones opposite Lil' James. The moment I sat down, I noticed Lil' James was smiling.

"What?" I asked,

"You know where I got this from, right?" He spoke. "Dorothy. She's crazy."

I burst into laughter, and a few seconds later, James and Lil' James joined in, too. It was easier to laugh, so much easier because if I didn't, I would be bawling my eyes out. My son didn't need that. He needed his parents to be strong.

When we finally collected ourselves, the doctor advised that Lil' James be returned to his room.

"See you later, Mom," he said as he walked to his room, and I did my best to hold back tears. After he left, James and I sat silently as the doctor rattled off words and symptoms, I wished I weren't listening to.

"Your son's been diagnosed with psychosis and bipolar," he said. "We think he's been taking the drugs to self-medicate."

Lil' James had confessed to them that he'd tried different drugs, including benzos, PCP, mushrooms, and bath salts. The more the doctor said, the less I heard because the only words echoing in my ears were, "You know where I got this from? Dorothy, she's crazy."

***

Dorothy was mentally unwell, but she was also a mom. And as a child, it was easier to see the mother who hurt me with her words and actions than the woman who was mentally ill and desperately needed help.

As an adult, I'd started to suspect Dorothy wasn't well. Her actions began to seem less like that of a bad mother and more like that of an unstable woman—someone constantly attacked by her mind and trauma but unable to fight back because she came from a long line of men and women who'd never been taught how, who saw seeking help as a form of weakness.

But even with this realization, the child in me was so hurt by her actions that the adult in me struggled to rationalize them.

I'd think of the woman who put my sisters and I out of the house in the cold, with plenty of anger and not enough warm clothes, and I got furious.

I'd think of her sunken silences and how, when she came out of them, she made us fight for her attention and get heartbroken.

I'd think of that time when she held the knife against my neck, and cry.

I knew some part of it was broken and that she didn't know how to put those pieces back herself, but I was still hurt. No matter how much the adult in me tried to explain to the child in me that she couldn't help it, that she didn't know what she was doing I was still so hurt.

Now, to see those broken pieces in my own child and to realize that the drugs and the loudness he'd so craved so badly was his way of fixing the pieces, so they didn't resemble my mother broke my heart.

Had God done this? Had He broken my son so that in fixing him I could see my mother clearer?

***

Lil' James began his treatment, but a week into it, he signed himself out and came back to the house in a murderous rage, screaming, cursing, and throwing things at us. When he calmed down, we managed to take him back to the hospital.

"Why did you let him leave?!" we asked. "Can't you see he's sick?! What is wrong with you people?!"

"We can't hold him here against his will, ma'am," they said. "He's eighteen. Legally an adult, and he can sign himself out whenever he wants. The only way we can have him committed is if he gives you power of attorney."

The next day, I had a lawyer draw up a power of attorney document and tried to get Lil' James to sign it, but he wouldn't. His sickness made him see everything I did as a scheme, a ploy, some tactic to destroy him. Somehow, I became the enemy, the one who had ruined his life and who was still trying to destroy it.

The more he attacked me, the more I begged him to take his medicine, to go to the hospital, to try to feel better again.

"Don't you want to feel better?" I asked in desperation.

"I don't like drugs," he said. "I don't like the hospital. I don't want to be there."

Eventually, he settled for an outpatient program that involved me or James dropping him off and picking him up after work. But his sessions finished before I closed from work and he had to stop by Rhoshay's to wait for me, an arrangement I had begged Rhoshay to agree to. That arrangement lasted three days before Rhoshay gave up.

"He's scaring my kids!" she called one day, "I can't have him here, Rhoda. You need to come get him."

He came back home, but it was more of the same weeks of him terrifying us, pretending to take his meds, leaving the house for days on end without a call until finally he just stopped coming home.

But now that I knew how sick he was, it was even more tortuous, sitting at home or at work wondering where he was, what he was doing. Was he hurting himself or someone? Was he ever going to get better?

One day, I was talking to Momma about it, and she said, "You know your great-grandfather was sick too. He was sick for years," she said. "Crazy in the head. Didn't know who I was half the time. Didn't know who I was until he died. Little wonder your Momma acts like she does sometimes. And Lil' James. It's not their fault," she said. "It's in our bloodline."

I thought then about her and her addiction to alcohol, her recent diagnosis, of Uncle Curtis and his addiction to heroin, Elijah and his bipolar, and Dorothy, I thought about Dorothy… Momma was right. It was in our bloodline.

And that's when it hit me; I should never have had children.

Chapter 19:
The Weight of Truth

While dealing with racism and microaggression at work, I got my Master's in Health Care Administration, and just as I'd hoped, I was able to get a top administrative position in one of the hospitals. I finally started to make enough for James to quit his job. I told him the moment I did, and as I anticipated, he had an excuse ready to go.

"We have got bills, Rhoda," he said.

"And I'll take care of them. I make enough now," I said. "That was the agreement."

"Yes, but we've still got debts. You'd barely be able to breathe paying it off on just your salary."

"James..."

"No," he said.

He was adamant, and I said nothing more about it. However, a few months later, James came home very hurt after being verbally attacked by his boss because of the number of complaints about some of the employees not doing their jobs with quality.

I saw the hurt and exhaustion in his eyes as he talked. That weary look of giving your best but still being undervalued and underappreciated for it and I just couldn't take it anymore. I knew exactly what that felt like.

"Resign tomorrow," I said.

"I can't do that," He replied. I understood what he meant. Even with my promotion, we were still dealing with the mortgage and several other bills. I was making more, but it still felt like we were broken somehow. But I could tell James wanted to quit. So, I pushed.

"Yes, you can. You don't need to go back there. We will manage. I will take care of us."

We sat there and talked some more about it, and the more we did, the more James warmed up to the idea.

Still, he was nervous, so he said, "But we will miss out on my paycheck."

"We are broken with your paycheck now," I replied. "So, it will not matter."

I typed up his resignation later the next morning, and that day, as he took it to go resign, he asked nervously, "Can we pray about it?"

"Of course," I said. I took his hand, and we prayed, asking the Lord to give us faith, to bless the decision we had made, and to open doors for James to do the work He intended for him.

When James tendered his resignation, his boss was shocked. He spent the next two weeks begging James to reconsider. That's how we knew just how valued James was. It took him wanting to resign for them to show him the respect he was always due. James turned down all their pleas.

"Thank you," he said, "But I'm going to ride into the sunset."

After his resignation, he poured himself into his remodeling business, and I poured myself into caring for Jaylen. But more than caring for him, I watched him for signs. Some days, when he wasn't home, I would go into his room to look around. I wasn't sure what I was looking for, but I'd lost one son, and I was terrified of losing another. Terrified that I would fail as a mother twice. Hating myself as I searched his room for signs and clues, but not being able to stop because what if lightning struck in the same place twice? Every time I didn't find anything, I got scared that he was hiding it better than I was finding it, and I would search even more. There were days when he came back from school, walked into his room, and walked back out a few minutes later with a look that let me know he knew; he knew that I'd been there looking for things. But he never said anything. It was as if he knew that I needed this, that searching and snooping was my strange way of proving my worth, of doing it right the second time. If I stayed on top of things this time, then he wouldn't turn out like his brother.

Searching became a way of redeeming myself from the failure I assigned myself from parenting Lil' James. Searching was, for me, a proactive and preventable strategy.

But the more I searched, the more I saw a kid desperate not to be like his brother. He was up and ready before the school bus came. He was home on time, never a minute late. His schoolwork was always done, and his grades were always good. At ten years old, he was not like other kids his age. He didn't play with the carefreeness with which they did. He was studious, sober, and careful. Never out of line, never talked back, never naughty. There were days when this worried me, when I feared that he wasn't being himself, where I was terrified that he was burying who he was to make space for who we needed him to be, but on those days, I would think of Lil' James and bury that fear—lightening was not going to strike in one place twice.

***

Lil' James stayed gone for two years. He lived in Arizona at that time, and while there, he would call and ask for money or food, and I would often send it to him. Those two years were hard. They were two years of despising myself for failing him, of hating the law that allowed Lil' James's permission to sign himself out even though he was clearly unwell. Two years of hating myself even more again because I should have seen it. I should have known. I was his mother. He came out of me. I should have known something wasn't right with him.

Those two years were heavy with words unsaid between James and I. I know though he never said it, he blamed himself just as much as I did. We had somehow bore a child that had taken the worst parts of our lineage, a child haunted by a sickness he knew nothing about. I thought of Lil' James as hapless. The odds hadn't been in his favor. I wondered if, given the chance, I would go back in time to undo Lil' James. But then I knew I'd lose all the precious moments, too, and there were many. Twelve years of them before he became someone else.

Somehow, and it was impossible not to notice, my sister's children had escaped it. Rhoshay had two kids, Rayneika had three, and Rayshaun had one, and sometimes when they came around, I would look at them closely, scrutinizing their behaviors, checking to see if they had picked it up too, but they seemed normal, healthy, happier than most kids. They had escaped it, but my son hadn't. It got harder to be around my nephew and nieces; harder to be around children at all because I couldn't look at them without thinking about Lil' James as a child.

I lost count of the nights I spent hoping and praying Lil' James would come back home. My prayers went unanswered. It was as if suddenly God did not care. He had saved me so many times. Why couldn't He save my son? Why didn't He want to?

I prayed and prayed. But just when it seemed like my prayers were forever going to remain unanswered, Lil' James came home.

He called me unexpectedly one day and begged me to send him money to come back to St. Louis. Without a second thought, I did.

He was a stranger when he returned. I was torn between relief at seeing him and fear of what he had become and what he might do. He had a beard and some scars on his face. It was clear, so clear he hadn't been taking his medication.

I wanted to ask him where he had been, what he had been doing, and if he was here to stay now. To get help? But he'd looked so beaten, so defeated, that I'd simply taken his bag and shown him to his room—the room I'd left exactly the same way he'd left it.

Jaylen was ten years old by now, and he looked at his brother with trepidation, staying as far away from him as he could. To him, Lil' James was even more of a stranger. James and I had at least known a different Lil' James, a happy, mischievous little boy. But all Jaylen knew of him was a brother who was mentally unstable and had caused so many tears for his mom.

The night Lil' James came back, Jaylen came to our bedroom as we prepared for bed and asked, "Mom, are we going to be safe with Lil' James here?"

I answered yes immediately while James looked at me skeptically.

"He used to threaten to drown me, you know."

James and I looked at him aghast.

"He used to do what?" James asked.

"When we both used to go to the basketball court by the lake, he used to say, 'I should throw you into that lake and let you drown.' I thought he was going to do it."

After Jaylen left our room, James said, "It's not a good idea for him to be here."

"He has nowhere else to be," I said. "Maybe we can help him get better this time, refill his medication, and finally get him to give us that power of attorney so we can have him committed."

"What about Jaylen?" James asked.

"We can't give up on Lil' James. He's our son, too."

I had Lil' James's prescription refilled the next day. He seemed thankful for them, and for a few days, he appeared to be taking them. Until we found out again, he wasn't. He was back to stealing things from the house and selling them for drugs.

Every time I confronted him, he'd lash out at me and say the meanest and most horrible things. Things that left me weak and heartbroken. The things he did paled in comparison to everything I'd been through before that. To have my child come at me like I was the enemy, determined to hurt me, left me paralyzed.

I thought I'd been stressed before; I thought I'd been through a lot, but Lil' James being home again was the most stressful period of my life. My skin broke out in hives, and the skin on my face dried up and began to peel. James tried to convince me to let him go then, but I couldn't; I wouldn't. I was not going to give up on him.

My skin continued to peel, and I called the doctor and explained my symptoms. "I can't go to work looking like this," I said. "My skin is so dry, it's peeling."

The doctor thought for a moment. "Have you started using any new products or changed your skincare routine recently?"

"No."

"How's work? Are you under stress?"

I hesitated for a moment. "Yes. But it's not from work." I told him all about Lil' James.

"Rhoda," he said sympathetically. "You need to let that go. It will kill you. Your body is already reacting to the stress."

"How am I supposed to let it go?" I asked. "He's, my son."

"I understand," he said. "How about therapy? I'll recommend someone to you."

I really didn't see myself spending hours on a couch, but I agreed. "Alright. Thank you."

"Take it easy," he said and hung up.

Lil' James left soon after that, and all I could think was I'd failed again until he showed up a few weeks later.

It was after midnight. I had finally fallen asleep after a restless tossing when I heard the banging on the door. James was out of bed before I fully registered what was going on. I followed him out of the bedroom, dreading what I knew I was going to find. It was Lil' James, banging, yelling, and cursing at me.

The rage in his voice was thick as if he'd been possessed by a thousand demons. One by one, the lights in the houses next to ours started to come on, and our neighbors, bleary-eyed with sleep, tied their ropes firmly around their waists and came out to watch the raging spectacle that was Lil' James.

I stood behind the closed door listening, and all I felt was shame, horror, and despair. His cusses and banging got louder, and James said in despair that matched mine, "We have to call the police officers. He is disturbing the entire street."

I'm not sure what I was about to say before Jaylen ran out, swinging a miniature baseball bat and crying. "I want a different big brother!" He screamed. "I want a different big brother!"

My heart broke as I walked to him and gently took the bat from him. His hands were shaking. He was so afraid.

"Call the police," I told James. He was already dialing.

The police arrived a few minutes later, with flashing lights and guns out, pointing at Lil' James, yelling at him to get down on the ground. He wouldn't. Instead, he turned to them in a rage and started to inch closer and closer toward them and their guns. All my fears flashed before my eyes, and I saw Lil' James dead on the floor.

"Get down!" they ordered, and he still wouldn't.

Somehow, my voice broke through the chaos. "Lil' James," I said calmly, even as everything inside me screamed. "Get on the ground before they are forced to hurt you."

As if pulled back by my voice, he immediately obeyed.

The police rushed forward and restrained him. We stayed inside as they spoke to him and finally convinced him to leave. After he left, one of the police officers approached us compassionately and said, "His behavior was a cry for help."

"We have done everything," I said. "We have tried everything we can to help him."

After they left, I knew then that I had to make a choice. I had to remove Lil' James from our lives to protect Jaylen. But I didn't know if I was strong enough to do it.

***

Lil' James returned a few days later, calmer. It was almost like, for him, that night hadn't happened. He seemed settled, and I watched him with trepidation. We went to church a few days later, and Lil' James, without much cajoling, went with us. A few people from the congregation expressed surprise at seeing

Lil' James again. Many couldn't hide their pity at his appearance, and a few openly prayed for him. Lil' James was calm the entire service, showing no indication of his usual rage or restlessness. But, on our way back home, as I drove 70 miles an hour on the highway, upset that I wouldn't buy him a plane ticket to Dallas, he got agitated.

"Pull over!" he yelled.

"Lil' James," I began, trying to appeal to him, "let's…"

"Pull over, or one of us is going to end up dead!"

I rushed to pull over, but before I could, he opened the car door, and in panic, I swerved. The energy in the car sharpened like cracks before a fire started, and in fear, I'd wanted to scream at Lil' James to close the damn door before he killed us all.

But Jaylen looked me straight in the eyes and said calmly, "Mom, just be quiet."

I locked eyes with Jaylen, nodded, and went deathly still, waiting and waiting and waiting, listening to Lil' James breathing heavily while the car door hung open. Somehow, I don't know how, Lil' James relaxed, shut the door, and went silent. We drove the rest of the way home in silence, and as we did, I went over the last few days in my head.

Jaylen, crying, terrified and swinging a baseball bat at his brother.

Jaylen, watching the police officers point a gun at his brother.

Jaylen, watching his brother cuss and attack me.

Jaylen, terrified of having his brother at home.

I wondered then how he slept at night. Did he go to sleep, terrified that Lil' James would sneak into his room and hurt him? Did he barricade his door? I was trying to save one son, but in doing that, I was sacrificing another. I held back tears as I realized this because I didn't want Jaylen to see me cry.

He had to go. This was it. Lil' James had to go.

When we got home, Lil' James raged and screamed and packed his things in a crazy frenzy. I said nothing as he did. I said nothing as he stormed out of the house and slammed the door. A heavy silence settled in the house after he left. This silence is still there now. It's light on some days and heavier on others, a constant reminder that a part of me is gone.

Lil' James never came back. That was the last time we saw him.

Chapter 20:
Facing the Hardest Truth

I looked at Dorothy with more compassion now, more empathy, more understanding. I tried to understand her moods and why she acted the way she did. I judged her less, even when her actions had nothing to do with her sickness—a sickness she'd never admit to having or seek help for because Black people don't do things like that.

I tried not to get angry when she mocked my relationship with Rhoshay. "Rhoshay be treating you like you her mother," she said jealously one time because Rhoshay had formed the habit of coming to me for advice or comfort. I didn't fault her for it. I would be jealous, too, if my child went to someone else for advice and comfort, even if that someone was a sibling. As a mom, you want to be the first person your child comes to when they are hurt or heartbroken. But you don't get to do that if you spent their life being the cause of their hurt and heartbreak.

All of us grew up taking what Dorothy could give and never expecting more. It was strange now that she faulted us for not asking for things she never gave.

My understanding of Dorothy and her moods led me to seek out Lil' James after he left again. Dorothy still managed to function, hold down a job, raise four daughters (albeit shabbily), and even buy a house. Surely Lil' James could too. I was still so desperate to save him. Despite his rejection of every help to get better, it felt so unfair to me, so unfair that this was happening to him. He didn't ask to be bipolar. No one would ever ask for this.

So, I inquired about his whereabouts and found out he had moved in with a friend's aunt. He was close by, I thought that was a win. Maybe instead of simply letting him go, I could try again to get that power of attorney from him. But I contacted the woman he was staying with and found out Lil' James wasn't there anymore.

"I couldn't have him here anymore," she said. "He was scaring me. I took him to his grandfather's."

Okay, I thought. He is with family, even better. Still, I thought about how that must be. His grandfather never really believed that he was as sick as we said. I worried that he had no idea what he was walking into. I found out when I called a week later that I was right.

"I couldn't take it anymore," Mr. Banks said. "I put him on a bus to Arizona."

My heart fell, "Why Arizona?"

"He says he's got a job there and a place to live."

"What?"

"This is good," he said quickly. "A job will keep him busy, keep him from spiraling out."

"There is no job," I said. "I wished you hadn't believed him. I wish you hadn't let him go. I needed him to give me power of attorney so I could have him committed."

"I'm sorry, Rhoda," he said.

"Me too."

※※※

With Lil' James in Arizona, I needed to know that he was alive and well. Someday, I hoped that he would seek help. That he would check into a treatment facility, that he would take his drugs, and work hard to be better, but until then, I felt the need and responsibility to keep him alive and well.

So, I began to send him money and supplies: food, clothes, groceries. I packed them in boxes and sent them to him. I only knew where to send these things because he called a few months after he left, in dire need of funds and sustenance. I was so relieved to hear his voice that I didn't think twice about sending him money. He was alive, and he kept in touch and that was what mattered to me.

James found out about my monthly supply to Lil' James and shook his head in disapproval.

"We have done everything we can for him. He's chosen this; let him live with it. He will come back to us when he's ready to get better."

But that only made me angry. Didn't he get it? Didn't he understand? Lil' James wouldn't come back. He was stubborn like Dorothy. He wouldn't come back even if he wanted to. His stubborn pride wouldn't let him. And how would he know to come back if I didn't stay in touch? Was I just supposed to move on? From what? From a child I carried in my belly for seven months? A child I'd almost died giving birth to. A child that was an extension of myself? How do you move on from a part of you that you are supposed to carry around forever?

So, I kept sending funds and supplies to him. Some part of me knew to stop, knew he was probably using the money for drugs and the supplies to trade for even more drugs. But I liked to think he wasn't. I wanted to believe he was taking care of himself. I kept sending and waking depressed every time he called to harass me for not sending more. Taking care of him like this was supposed to give me peace of mind, absolve me of the guilt of letting him go.

Instead, it troubled my mind and increased my stress. My face went back to peeling again, and this time, I knew not to call my doctor, but I wasn't sure what to do until the employee assistance counselor at work suggested therapy.

"In person this time," she said when I told her I'd done one over call.

I didn't want to. I didn't trust myself to sit in front of a therapist without crying my eyes out. I was too ashamed and embarrassed to do that. But what else was I going to do? I knew I needed to do it. I needed to do it for Jaylen.

My therapist was a nice, competent woman who tried to get me to relax on our first session, but I couldn't. I sat nervously on her couch as if I were expecting any member of my extended family to walk in and find me conversing with a therapist. She tried to get me to open up about Lil' James, about Dorothy, about work, but I sat there, evading and counting down the minutes until I could leave.

Eventually, because Lil' James was the bane of my existence, I started to talk about him. I talked about him slapping his brother and being found at a drug house at 12, skipping school, smoking pot, stealing my car, stealing my money, jewelry, liquor, staying away from home for days on end, moving out to live with some White family in a trailer and finally getting diagnosed.

By the time I got to the incident with the police officers, the car, and Jaylen swinging a baseball bat, I was crying.

"It's been a nightmare," I cried. "He rejected all our help. He's somewhere in Arizona now, and all I can do is send him money."

"You give him money?" the therapist said.

"Yes..."

"You need to stop sending money."

"What?"

"He uses your money to buy drugs, to feed his habit. Do you want him to OD?" She asked.

My blood turned cold. "Of course not. I was… I didn't…"

"Then stop giving him money."

"But what is he going to do if I don't give him money? How is he going to survive."

"I know this is hard to hear right now, but that is not your problem anymore. He needs to want to get better for himself."

"How is that not my problem?! He's my son."

"Yes. And if he ODs because you kept giving him money, money he was using to buy drugs, you will never forgive yourself."

I sighed in defeat. "I don't know what to do."

"You can start by letting go of the guilt," she said. "His choices are not a reflection of your parenting. He has choices, and he is choosing the wrong things. He is not the same Lil' James you raised. He has evolved to be the person he chose to be."

The therapist's words settled in my mind, and I thought about them all the way home. By the time I parked the car, I was no closer to letting go of the guilt. But she was right about one thing. I needed to stop sending him money. I already blamed myself for so much, I couldn't add his possible death to it.

I avoided Lil' James's calls for days, and when I finally got the courage to tell him I wouldn't be sending him any more money or supplies, he stopped calling me. I lost that little piece of connection.

❋❋❋

I poured myself into work again.

I finally got into Human Resource Training and Development at the hospital I worked at. I became the Director of Learning and

Innovation. I had the opportunity to design learning experiences for healthcare providers. Finally, it felt like I was working in my purpose, helping others reach their full potential, pouring into others through learning experiences, teaching them how to be better leaders, and how to inspire their employees to provide exceptional patient care, whether it required billing or treating them.

However, as much as I loved my job, it was particularly challenging. I was very often the only Black woman in a room full of other senior leaders, and that meant often facing microaggressions. Some of my colleagues would either say things that were hurtful, triggering, or inappropriate.

For instance, one time, while providing feedback on a Black female employee who had acted inappropriately in a meeting, the White female executive I was giving the feedback to had scrunched up her face and asked, "Is that a Black girl thing?"

I looked at her in bewilderment. Was it a Black girl thing to be rude or inappropriate during meetings? To be unprofessional? Is that what she was asking me?

"It's a people thing," I said. And she'd had the grace to at least look embarrassed.

Another time, after being asked by our Chief HR officer to facilitate a senior executive offsite, that senior executive asked in the most condescending tone, "What qualifies you to lead our session?"

But the one that really hurt was when the only senior Black female leader told me she couldn't be seen with me because she didn't want the White people at the office to say she was only helping people who looked like her. To drive home her point, she removed herself from a table we were both sitting at in a meeting to avoid triggering that perception. A perception White people don't even have to worry or think about themselves.

However, despite all this, when it came to my work, I had a drive to win, stand out, give my all, and do better. And that was hard to ignore.

So, it wasn't long before I was promoted again and put in charge of a project at work. By this time, Jaylen was in high school, and James's remodeling business was doing well. He was doing great at it as I predicted. In his first year, he made double his salary working for himself than he did overseeing a department of fifty people. He was so busy he had customers on a waiting list.

Everything was well with us. Slowly, we'd learned to move on from Lil' James. I still carried the gaping hole of his absence in my heart everywhere I went, but it was getting easier to get out of bed in the morning. I leveraged my faith in God to cope. I continued to believe no matter how far away he was from me; he was never too far from God. I believed that he would show up one day a clean man, well-shaven, and in his right mind.

I believe that God will put people in his life to help him, and he will receive the help he needs. I'll continue to believe this until proven otherwise.

To believe anything else is paralyzing.

I continued to take life and work day by day. All was well until death almost took me.

We were implementing a new electronic health record, and I was the director of the training program for the use of electronic health record technology. We named the project Epic. Implementing Epic was challenging. I spent a lot of time traveling and a ton of hours trying to build the training program. So, when I first started to fall sick, I attributed it to stress.

I went to my primary healthcare provider that first week and complained of fever and frontal headaches. I was on high blood pressure medicine at the time. The doctor, without running any tests, concluded I had a sinus infection and prescribed me penicillin. I took the drugs diligently and noticed a week later that my urine was very dark. I thought about going back to the hospital but decided against it. It was probably a virus, nothing serious.

Weeks passed, and I started becoming sicker and weaker. Eventually, I was unable to eat or keep food down. I was constantly running a fever and feeling dizzy. Deciding that this was more than a virus, I went to the emergency room and explained my symptoms. They gave me a prescription for more antibiotics, again without running any tests or doing any bloodwork.

"Can you run some tests?" I asked my doctor. "I really don't like how I feel."

"You'll be fine," she said. "Just take your antibiotics."

I went home, took the antibiotics, and continued to fall sicker and sicker. My body was becoming weaker and weaker. I went back to my primary care doctor; certain she would run tests now. She had to; my body felt like it was shutting down on me. When I got there, looking pale and feeling weaker than I had in months, I listed my symptoms to her and waited for her to order some lab tests for me. Instead, she said, "You need to lose weight, Rhoda. You will feel much better once you do."

I was too stunned to speak. My weight had escalated after the birth of Lil' James. People looked at me and assumed I spent all my time eating, but I didn't. I ate normal portions but kept gaining weight and had no idea how to lose it. I knew, deep down, my symptoms had nothing to do with my weight because, during the duration of my sickness, I had lost 40 pounds. But I took the set of drugs she prescribed and left. She was the doctor; she had to know what she was talking about.

It turned out she didn't.

By the next week, I was unable to keep water down. Every time I drank it, I threw up. A few days later, I woke up and nearly blacked out before I left the bed. In a panic, James rushed me to the hospital. I was barely responsive now, and they had to run tests. After they did, a doctor came in and said soberly, "Mrs. Banks, you are in kidney failure."

The room went silent, and I shook my head vehemently.

"No, I don't want that," I said. Something in me moved, and I started praying and speaking in tongues. The doctor shuffled his feet uncomfortably and left the room. I ignored that and kept praying.

My kidneys are not failing, I prayed. My kidneys are not failing.

A little while later, another doctor walked in and exclaimed excitedly when he saw me.

"Hey!" he said. "It's the Epic Lady!"

My work with Epic was so impressive and monumental that it gave me something of a celebrity status in the medical space. Our project was due to receive recognition because of how well our implementation of it had gone. I was going to receive an honorable mention from the CEO and Owner of the Electronic Health Record vendor because of how exceptional our training program was.

"Why are you here?" the doctor asked.

Grateful to have someone give me this level of attention, I spoke to him anxiously. "I blacked out this morning, and my husband brought me in. The other doctor says my kidneys are failing."

He turned to the nurse next to him, "Have the lab run more tests. She's the Epic Lady. Let's find out what exactly is going on."

They ran more tests and found out my kidneys were indeed shutting down. They have been since the week I walked into my physician's office, and she prescribed me penicillin. Everyone was stunned. "Why didn't you say something?" they asked.

"Your body has become toxic because your kidneys stopped working," the Doctor said. "If you had waited one more hour to get here, you would have died."

James and I were speechless.

"Surely you noticed something?" the doctor asked, perplexed. "Your urine getting dark? Throwing up? Being unable to keep food or water down?"

"She went to her doctor," James said angrily. The anger and fear in his voice reverberated throughout the room. "She went, and they told her to lose weight."

The doctors and nurses went quietly.

"What's going to happen now?" I asked.

"We are going to insert a PICC line to flush you out," the doctor said. "I don't want to scare you, but we might have to put you on dialysis if the PICC line is unable to clear your body of the toxins."

I began to cry because this was the second time in my life my kidneys were failing. Why did death seem to have a fondness for me? I didn't want to die, not without seeing my son again. But I cried harder because I felt like that was it for me. I'd escaped death so many times before, it seemed fitting it'd take me now.

I got furious at my primary physician. I told her. I told her something wasn't right. She had treated my symptoms with such nonchalance, dismissed it completely like I was bothering her, and she had better patients to attend to. They are taking good care of me now. Giving me the attention and care I needed. But what if I wasn't the Epic lady? What if I was just another Black woman who came in here almost dead? Would they have attended to me? Wouldn't I already be dead?

James called my sisters and Momma to inform them. They expressed their shock and asked what they could do. Momma, of course, did the only thing she knew to do pray. James brought Jaylen, too. He sat in my hospital room, just watching and waiting.

When James called Dorothy and she came to see me, I cried. I was so touched and thankful she had come. We were in a much better place now. This wasn't like the first time with Lil' James. I knew she would say the right thing. But instead, she said matter of factly, "There's no point crying, Rhoda. If it's your time to go, then it's your time to go."

I wasn't sure whether to weep in disappointment or order her out in anger. She left and didn't come to see me again until I left the hospital.

The next day, the doctors informed me they wanted to do a biopsy on my kidneys. I cried softly as the radiologist wheeled me to the biopsy. Biopsy meant cancer to me, and I was afraid they would find something else.

The radiologist wheeling me to the biopsy paused when he noticed me crying. He knelt next to me and whispered in my ears. "Sweetheart, don't cry. This is not unto death. The kidneys are resilient."

Confused by the manner in which he spoke, I looked at him with tear-filled eyes, and he nodded with a smile. "Your kidneys are resilient," he repeated. Without waiting for me to say anything, he got up and continued to wheel me.

I felt peace settle over me after that. And I remember thinking that he had to be an angel because what normal person talks like that? I asked about him after my biopsy, and on the day, I was checking out of the hospital. They had no idea about whom I was talking to. I still believe he was an angel.

My biopsy results came back negative.

"Your kidneys are going to be fine. It's a miracle!" the doctor said. "When we measured your kidneys that first time to see how well they were working, the creatinine level showed seventeen. That's insane! A normal creatinine level is 0.0001, and any normal person would have needed dialysis or died when theirs reached a level of six. Yours got to seventeen! 17! I don't know how you are here right now. But this is an absolute miracle!"

I was also told that I had an allergic reaction to the penicillin my primary physician prescribed. That, along with the blood pressure medicine, caused an adverse reaction with the penicillin.

"Only five percent of people in the world have this type of allergic reaction, particularly one that impacts the kidneys. We are recommending a new blood pressure medicine for you, and you can never take penicillin ever again."

I walked out of that hospital five days later, knowing God had more planned for my life. While my doctor had been ignoring my symptoms, God had been sustaining me. I remembered then that when I was sick and wondering what was wrong, I could hear the Lord's voice internally saying: "I am the core of your existence. In Me, you live, and in Me, you move, and in Me, you have your being."

I have no idea why, once again, I didn't die, but I intend to live fully. And maybe, perhaps, one day, I'll see my son again.

Chapter 21:
The Winds of Change

Dorothy lost her house.

First, it started to break down. She had the basement flooding in the winter, the AC breaking down, and the heater not working. I helped her as much as I could. I paid to fix the heater and gave her some money for other minor repairs, but the house kept breaking down. It seemed the more Dorothy loved and took care of it, the more it was determined to break her heart.

Soon, the many repairs in the house started to affect paying her mortgage. But Dorothy was intent on keeping the house. She worked harder than I'd ever seen to keep up with payments. I was impressed by it, by her determination to fight to keep something she loved. I loved seeing her fight because I'd seen her give up easily many times before.

She continued to fight for her home until it got broken into. Some teenagers in the neighborhood broke into her house, went through her stuff, used her toilet without flushing, left a mess in her kitchen, and stole her stuff. She was furious when she found out, just like she'd been when she found out Eric stole her photos. When she confronted them in rage, they responded with, "So what? You don't even have any stuff."

That had enraged her even more. The teenagers had rudely laughed in her face, and I couldn't help but think they would have trembled before a younger Dorothy. Eric definitely had after Dorothy blazed in and demanded her naked pictures.

Dorothy gave up on the house after that. It was as if those kids had violated something she held precious, and she could no longer look at it the same way. The bank repossessed the house, and she moved back into an apartment.

The house wasn't the only thing she lost.

***

Rayneika could no longer cope, so we urged Dorothy to take Momma in. It seemed like a convenient set-up; Dorothy was living alone, and Momma needed companionship. But Dorothy didn't want to take her in.

"I don't want her living in my house," she said. But she relented after we begged, and eventually, Momma moved in. However, Dorothy wasn't much of a companion to her. She still shut herself up during family conversations, doing it more now because Momma lived with her. She even refused to invite Momma to her birthday trip we organized for her. I organized the trip and suggested we bring Momma along and Dorothy had snapped at me before I even finished the sentence.

"It's my birthday!" she said. "I don't want her to come."

Momma had taken it in good faith. She needed Dorothy now and wasn't about to upset her. But none of us could have foreseen Dorothy would be the one needing her very soon.

When Dorothy turned sixty-two, a few weeks before Christmas, she started complaining of back pain. It started out small, and soon, it was a throbbing, aggravating pain. Unable to bear it anymore, she asked Rhoshay to take her to the emergency room. When they got there, the doctors ran tests and soberly told Dorothy they had discovered a large mass in her lungs. Dorothy had sat there uncomprehending the word mass while Rhoshay burst into tears.

Unable to handle the news herself, she called me crying, "I think Dorothy has lung cancer." Much like me, Rhoshay didn't have the best relationship with Dorothy, even more so after I left. But I could feel her heartbreak through the phone when she uttered those words. She was devastated.

I'd been too shocked to say anything. It seemed cruel that Dorothy would be getting this type of news during her favorite holiday.

"Let's take her to a specialist," I said after I'd calmed Rhoshay. "We need to be sure."

I scheduled a meeting with a specialist for the coming week. If this were really cancer, I wanted Dorothy to get a head start immediately, and if it weren't, I wanted her to get peace of mind so she could enjoy her favorite holiday.

When we got there, the specialist confirmed what we feared. "It's lung cancer," he said. "And from the size of it, it's been growing for eight years."

Rhoshay gasped in shock, and I burst into tears. Beside me, Dorothy sat deathly still.

The doctor looked from me to her and sighed wearily. "I'm really sorry," he said. "I urge you to go see an oncologist. But you might as well wait to see the oncologist after the holidays because nothing's going to change this situation between now and then.

The specialist excused himself and left, and as we walked out of the hospital, Dorothy said, "Let's go get breakfast."

Through the haze of my tears, I looked at her in confusion. "Are you sure?"

"I'm not trying to stay here and hear all this," she said. "Let's go get breakfast."

So, we left, and I took Dorothy to her favorite breakfast spot. I watched her eat with gusto, spooning food after food into her mouth like she hadn't just heard the worst news of her life. I wanted to say something, but I didn't. I simply watched her eat and tried to remember a time when she'd enjoyed food like this.

The holiday passed with Dorothy showing her usual holiday spirit. I watched her with worry and surprise. Why was she acting like all was well? Like she hadn't been hit with devastating news? I was barely getting through the holiday, but she was acting fine.

A few weeks into the new year, I called Dorothy to remind her about seeing an oncologist.

"I'm not trying to do no treatment," she said. "I'm fine." She coughed for a minute after she said that, and I had to hold the phone away.

"You are not fine," I said softly. "But the treatment will make you better."

"Will it?" she asked.

I said nothing to that.

✷✷✷

I traveled less after Dorothy became sick. Rhoshay and I reworked our schedules so one of us could be available to take her for treatment. We got together and worked out a timetable on how to get her to and from the hospital, and on all those days, Dorothy insisted on having breakfast at her favorite breakfast place first.

We tried to get our younger sisters, Rayneika and Rayshaun, to participate, but they weren't as available. At first, I was angry with them until I realized not being available was a coping mechanism—

ignore a situation and perhaps it will go away. But it was clear they were very afraid for Dorothy. Everyone seemed to be more afraid for Dorothy than she was for herself.

During Thanksgiving at my place, every time Uncle Curtis was over with his wife, Dorothy found a reason to cuss at him. It didn't matter what he said or how he said it; she found a way to cuss at him. And every time Momma tried to get in the mix, she cussed harder at her too. Uncle Curtis never tried to defend himself when she got like this; he simply stood there and took it. He knew why she was angry, even if Momma refused to acknowledge it.

What he did to her, the beatings and attacks always remained unspoken between Dorothy, Momma, and Uncle Curtis after he got saved. But it was always there in their eyes, in the discomfort of Momma's when Dorothy and Uncle Curtis were in the same room together, in the anger in Dorothy's every time she looked at both of them, and in the guilt in Uncle Curtis's.

So, when Dorothy got sick, Momma and Uncle Curtis saw it as an opportunity to make up for what they had done and didn't do. Momma tended to Dorothy just as she had done to Bill, and whenever Rhoshay and I couldn't get time away from our schedules, Uncle Curtis would come to pick Dorothy up and take her to her treatments.

Dorothy let them. She stopped being mean to Momma and didn't cuss at Uncle Curtis any longer. It was as if she'd suddenly let go of the anger she had toward them, and in turn, they saw taking care of her as penance.

Dorothy kept up her treatments steadily. It was aggressive. She was getting radiation and chemo at once to shrink the cancer. Three times a week, we would drive her and watch her get hooked up to the machines to get her treatment. She hated the treatment, hated how they made her feel afterward, too weak to sit up or care for her plants. It upset her, I could tell, but I never saw her cry. Instead, she sat stoically on her chair, browsing through a magazine. She didn't acknowledge the cancer or the treatments; it was a thing that wasn't happening to her.

The trajectory of her treatment was a heartbreaking one.

She completed her chemo and radiation and rang the bell of victory. I remember the look on her face that day. It was one of disbelief and joy. I realized then that, of course, she had been anxious and afraid. Ignoring it was also her way of dealing with it. We all went out to dinner to celebrate. It was the happiest I'd seen Dorothy in a long time. But a few months later, after going for post-chemo and radiation check-ups, she found out the cancer was still growing.

"I'm going to put you on an experimental pill," the doctor said. "But it's very expensive."

Desperate, Dorothy got on it. Thankfully, her insurance covered the payments. Unable to work, she saw how much of a good thing it was that Momma lived with her because Momma's retirement and savings helped pay rent and take care of the bills. To cheer them up, I organized a trip to Tunica, Mississippi, to visit Momma's family. Most of Momma's family were dead, but the ones alive were happy to see them. Before long, there was a family reunion going on, with a barbecue in the middle. I had visited before, but it was nice to visit again and hear new stories about Momma.

Later in the week, I took Momma and Dorothy to the casinos, and they gambled to their hearts' content, not caring that they were losing far more than they were winning. We had so much fun and on the day we left, I promised to bring them back again, along with Rhoshay.

"We will make it an even bigger trip," I said.

Dorothy took the experimental drugs for a few months, getting weaker as she did until the doctor informed her the pill wasn't working.

"Let's get you back on chemo," he said.

We went right back to it, taking turns to take her to the hospital. I tried to stay hopeful, but it was hard. Dorothy showed no signs of improvement. A few months into her second cycle of chemo, she had a seizure and was rushed to the emergency room.

We all met her there, and the doctor soberly informed her that the cancer had spread to her brain.

"What's next?" She asked, and I saw desperate hope in her eyes. But it died as the doctor shook his head.

"I'm sorry," he said. "There's nothing more we can do."

I started to cry, but Dorothy hardened her eyes and turned her face away. Still, I saw a single tear slide down her cheek. "I should have kept smoking," she said.

The doctor walked out of the room in disappointment. I was still crying when a nurse walked in. My tears made her mistake me for the patient, and Dorothy, completely disgusted, said, "Can you believe I'm the patient? You would think it was her. I should have left her at home."

The nurse smiled sadly and proceeded to tend to Dorothy. After she was done, still crying, I asked, "Well, do you still want to go to breakfast?"

"Heck yeah," she said. "What's the big deal?"

Again, I stared at her as she spooned food into her mouth. If it had been me and a doctor had just told me I was dying, I wouldn't have been able to eat.

***

Through her year-long treatment, Dorothy had remained in denial, acting like she wasn't deathly sick, even after the doctor told her there was nothing more he could do.

"I recommend hospice," he had said. "All we can do is keep her comfortable now."

Dorothy had ignored those words even then, but I finally saw a look of concern on her face when the hospice social worker came over to the house to explain the dying process to us. They would send a nurse three times a week to make sure Dorothy was comfortable. They also gave us a purple book to read. It described all the things we would notice the closer she got to death and what to do after she passed.

We all listened patiently and soberly, but Dorothy lay on her bed and listened with an air of detachment like none of this had anything to do with her. When the social worker was done talking, Dorothy asked, "So, what if I get better?"

Tears filled my eyes when she asked that, and the social worker looked at Dorothy compassionately. "Then you won't need hospice," she said.

"Okay," Dorothy said and turned her head toward the muted TV. We had arranged her bed, so it had a generous view of it.

As she got ready to leave, the social worker asked me if she could speak to me downstairs. I said sure and followed her. She explained even more of the process to me. I listened attentively, not fully accepting it myself. The thought of losing Dorothy was breaking my heart, and I wasn't sure how to deal with it. I went back inside after the social worker left, and Dorothy asked nervously, "what did she want?"

"Nothing," I said. "You rest now."

✶✶✶

Dorothy declined quickly, but there were days when she felt good. On those days, she would call me up in the middle of work and say, "They say I'm dying, but I don't feel like I am."

I'd hear the denial ringing in her voice and wonder what it felt like to simply be waiting to die.

Then she'd say, "At least if I die, I ain't got to pay bills no more."

Dorothy had spent all her life worrying about paying her bills. It was a constant, draining worry for her. I remember after she moved into her house, she called me one day and said, "Rhoda, I just paid all my bills, and I only got $10 dollars left." She sounded so depressed when she said that, so I said, "Wow! A whole $10!"

And she'd said, "What do you mean a whole $10?"

And I'd said, "You got money left from your paycheck after taking care of your bills. You've got a roof over your head, food, and your health. Girl, some people don't even have a paycheck."

She'd gone quiet and then said, "I never thought about it like that."

Eventually, Dorothy reached the point where she couldn't walk anymore. But that was when she decided to do as much movement as possible. Every time we came to see her, she would try to get us to help her to stand. And every time we did, she ended up collapsing back down. Her throat started to close up, making it hard to talk or breathe. Still, she lay in bed, talking to spirits we couldn't see and asking strange questions we didn't understand. Her behavior confused and saddened us, but we understood they were all part of the dying process.

I saw her fear in those moments. I saw her struggling to stay when it was so clear her body wanted to go. Sometimes, she would go very still and quiet, and in fear, I would ask, "Dorothy, are you leaving us?"

And she would say, "I don't know. I can't tell. They say that my robe isn't ready for me yet."

"Who's not ready for you yet?"

"My robe."

"What robe?"

But she wouldn't be able to explain it.

I talked to her about God a lot then. I tried to get her to repent before she left. All her life, she had never said she believed in God, but she never said she didn't either. But she was afraid, so afraid of where she was going next. And I'd say, "Don't be afraid, Dorothy. Just ask the Lord to receive your spirit unto Him. Just ask Him to forgive you."

And she said in a calm voice, "Rhoda, I know you think me and God don't have a relationship, but we cool. We cool."

"Then don't be afraid," I said." "Because where you are going is peaceful. It's beautiful, and you wouldn't want to come back here."

And she replied with the saddest smile I'd ever seen, "Not ever."

A week before Dorothy died, she woke up and asked to see a friend of hers, Deborah Buckley.

"I want to see Deborah Buckley," she kept saying. "I really want to see Deborah Buckley."

But she had cut off communications with Deborah years ago, so long ago that it took me a while to remember who she was talking about. After I did, I remembered that Deborah had a daughter named Tonya. I went online to search for her, and when I found her, she brought her mother to us. Deborah was just as old as Dorothy, but with kind eyes and still as gorgeous as I remembered her. She cried when she came and saw Dorothy because so many years had gone by. She sat by Dorothy's side, tending and talking to her.

After Deborah, we began to invite people from Dorothy's past to come see her. Some were happy to come, some called, some sent text messages to her phone, and some Dorothy didn't care to see, like Ray.

Ray had been out of prison for years, but no one knew where he was. So, when he walked into Dorothy's room on the Friday before Easter Sunday with our younger sister, Rayneika, me, Momma, Rhoshay, Rayshaun, Uncle Curtis, and his wife, all looked on in stunned silence.

"He's here to apologize," Rayneika said.

But Dorothy turned at that moment, saw him, stiffened, and grabbed my hand. "Rhoda," she said. "Get my shit." She meant her gun.

Her breathing became shallow, and I could feel her heart racing. I wanted to tell Ray to get out, but Rayneika stood next to him adamantly. He was her father, and I knew if I ordered him out, it would cause more commotion.

So, I looked into Dorothy's eyes and told her to breathe. "He's just here to apologize," I said. "And I'll be right outside the door."

As I walked past Ray, he looked me up and down and said with a smirk, "Y'all got big." I knew he was referring to my weight.

A few minutes after I walked out, there was a lot of screaming. Rayshaun was screaming at Rayneika for bringing Ray. As the chaos raged on, the hospice nurse pulled me aside.

"You need to get all these people out of here," she said.

"I can't just order them to leave," I said. "They are family just as much as I am."

"That's exactly what you need to do. Dying is hard work. Your mother will not pass with all these people screaming over her. I can tell she's a very private person."

I came back in to see that Rayneika had broken down in tears from the argument she had just had with Rayshaun. Everyone was gathered in Momma's room while Ray was in the room with Dorothy. There was no screaming coming from there, but I looked in to make sure. Ray was sitting next to Dorothy's bed, speaking softly to her.

The air was still charged, so rather than order everyone out, I led them all in prayer. That brought an air of calmness to the house. After Ray finished with Dorothy, Rayneika quietly took him home. I went back into the room to check on Dorothy, and when I asked her what Ray said, she answered, "he just kept apologizing."

"Good," I said.

I didn't let anyone else bother Dorothy after that.

Chapter 22:
A Final Goodbye

Dorothy died on Easter Sunday at 5:13 a.m.

The week of her death, we all camped at her apartment—all the children and grandchildren, except for Jaylen, who stayed home with James. The night before her death, Momma sat in the room watching Dorothy while the rest of us slept. By 5:00 a.m., she woke me up to take over.

"I can't take it anymore," she said.

I understood. Dorothy's breathing had become strained and labored. Each breath she breathed rattled painfully. I sat watching as Momma left the room, and a few minutes later, Rayshaun came in. She had just gotten off work. We sat talking about some stuff I can't remember now when suddenly, we heard the softest "Momma" from Dorothy.

We paused and turned to look at her. The rattling had stopped, and her chest had stilled. Her life had ended.

Rayshaun and I began to cry softly. Rhoshay walked quickly into the room, saw us crying, and raced to the bathroom in tears.

Momma came in, walked over to Dorothy, bent over, and looked at her face. She strengthened slowly, closed her eyes, opened them, and said, "Ya'll don't cry. She's no longer in pain."

Everyone in the house was crying except for Momma, but the pain in her eyes was palpable. I remember thinking that if she could stay strong after losing her only daughter, I could stay strong, too. I dried my eyes and made the necessary calls.

Dorothy wouldn't have cared for all the crying anyway.

❋❋❋

Dorothy didn't have a funeral. She had told me weeks earlier she didn't want anything that even resembled a funeral.

"I don't care for that," she said. "I don't care for that at all. I don't want people to look down on me. Just burn me up."

"And the ashes, what do you want us to do with it?"

"You can flush them down the toilet for all I care."

Of course, I had no intention of doing that. We cremated and split her ashes up between the four of us and Momma, and Momma, had cradled her urn tenderly and placed it gently on her shelf.

Afterward, we held a picnic in Dorothy's honor and invited all her childhood friends. Renee, who had driven Dorothy to the prison to marry Ray, was there too. She and Dorothy had stayed friends and grown closer as they aged. Momma still didn't cry, not through all the kind words and tributes to Dorothy. Not even when we released balloons in Dorothy's honor. They sailed up, up, up until they became dotted specks in the sky.

As we packed up the picnic, Renee sought me out. "You know Dorothy was very proud of you."

A lump formed in my throat. "She was?"

"Yeah. She bragged about you all the time. She was so proud of you and all you accomplished."

I thanked her, went home, and cried into my pillow.

A few weeks later, I got a call from an old classmate of Lil' James. She was working as a nurse in prison, and she just wanted to let me know that he was alive. I hadn't seen Lil' James in six years or heard from him in five. Sometimes, I'd go online to search for him. The last time I did, the picture I saw broke my heart. With vacant eyes, broken teeth, bushy hair, and flaky skin, he'd looked nothing like himself. I'd broken down in tears and promised myself not to search for him again. Seeing him like that hurt more than not seeing him at all.

To hear this young woman tell me about him now was a relief. I was thankful he was still alive, even though hearing about him being in prison broke my heart.

"He's in prison?" I asked.

"Yes. But he's well. He wants you to know he's doing okay."

"Okay. Thank you."

"Mrs. Banks," she said before I hung up. "I'm sure you did everything you could."

I smiled sadly. "Thank you."

After that, I got a couple of postcards from Lil' James with notes asking how everyone was and what he promised to do when he got out of prison. Those notes were like a lifeline; they kept me connected to my son, and they lessened my sadness. Still, every time I got one, I couldn't help but think of what the nurse had said. Was she right? Had I done the best I could?

Then I thought of Dorothy and all her demons and how I'd hated her when I was a child without fully knowing who she was and all the trauma she'd lived through. She had been a terrible mother, but she had done the best she could. In many ways, she was a victim, stuck in a cycle she didn't know how to get out of.

"She didn't fight," Rhoshay said after she died. "She should have fought harder. She was weak."

Maybe she was. But I believe she fought in the ways she could. And I hope Lil' James is doing the same.

Chapter 23:
Embracing Our Shadow

I stood in front of my mirror one morning, tracing the lines of my face—the same face Dorothy once called ugly, the same eyes that watched my father's funeral when I was five, the same determined jaw that helped me survive. For years, I'd avoided really looking at myself, afraid of what I'd see. Afraid I'd see Dorothy's rage or my father's violence etched into my features. But that morning was different. I saw strength in those lines. I saw survival. I saw hope.

My story began in the shadows of Carr Square Village, where violence and poverty shaped daily life. I was the daughter of an assassin, raised by a mother whose love was as unpredictable as her moods. I became a teenage breadwinner, a young wife, and eventually a mother trying desperately not to repeat the cycles that had shaped me.

Then I became a mother who had to let her son go, learning the hardest lesson of all—that sometimes love means accepting what we cannot change.

But my story didn't end in those shadows.

Each challenge I faced became a critical moment – a moment for opportunity. Every time Dorothy's words tried to break me, I built myself back stronger. When my father's legacy threatened to define me, I chose to define myself. When my son's illness tested everything I believed about motherhood and love, I learned that healing doesn't always look the way we expect it to.

I rose from a cashier in the hospital parking garage to serving in executive leadership, obtaining two master's degrees, and building a life bursting with purpose. Not because I was special or extraordinary, but because I refused to let my past dictate my future. James and I have stayed married for over three decades, breaking the cycle of unstable relationships that plagued both our families. We raised Jaylen in a home filled with love and stability—proof that patterns can be broken, that healing is possible.

Yet even now, success doesn't mean freedom from pain. I still carry the weight of Lil' James's absence. I still feel the echo of Dorothy's words sometimes. But I've learned that our shadows—those dark parts of our story we wish we could erase—are actually part of what makes us whole.

To you, reading these words, I want you to know this: Your past may explain you, but it doesn't have to define you. The cycles of trauma, addiction, and pain that run through our families are not our destiny unless we choose to make them so. Every day, we have the choice to write a new chapter.

I think about Dorothy now, in her final days, telling me "we cool" when I asked about her relationship with God. I think about Lil' James, somewhere out there, carrying pieces of all of us within him. I think about Momma, who survived her own demons to become the grandmother who helped hold us all together. Their stories live within mine—the pain, the triumph, the love, the loss—all of it creating the tapestry of who I am.

This memoir isn't just about surviving trauma or breaking cycles. It's about embracing every part of our story—even the shadows—because they show us how far we've come. It's about understanding that healing isn't a destination but a journey that continues with each generation.

To my sons, Lil' James and Jaylen, who taught me different kinds of love and different kinds of strength: Your stories are still being written. To those still struggling in the shadows: Your light is waiting to emerge. To everyone carrying the weight of generational trauma: You have the power to change the narrative.

Our shadows don't disappear—they become part of who we are. But they don't have to darken our future. They can instead remind us of our resilience, our capacity for growth, and our ability to transform pain into purpose.

This is how we heal. This is how we grow. This is how we turn our shadows into light.

With love and hope for your journey,
Rhoda

www.ingramcontent.com/pod-product-compliance
Lightning Source LLC
Chambersburg PA
CBHW070532170426
43200CB00011B/2405